THE IDIOM ADVANTAGE

FLUENCY IN SPEAKING AND LISTENING

DANA WATKINS

Addison-Wesley Publishing Company
Reading, Massachusetts • Menlo Park, California
New York • Don Mills, Ontario • Wokingham, England
Amsterdam • Bonn • Sydney • Singapore • Tokyo
Madrid • San Juan • Paris • Seoul, Korea • Milan
Mexico City • Taipei, Taiwan

The Idiom Advantage: Fluency in Speaking and Listening

Photo credits: Credits appear on page 240.

Editorial Director: Joanne Dresner
Acquisitions Editor: Allen Ascher
Development Editor: Françoise Leffler
Production Editor: Liza Pleva
Text Design and Production: Curt Belshe
Production Technical Assistant: Karen Philippidis
Cover Design: Joeseph DePinho
Text Art: Sarah Sloane

Library of Congress Cataloging in Publication Data
Watkins, Dana.
    The idiom advantage / Dana Watkins.
      p.   cm.
    ISBN 0-201-82527-9 (pbk.)
    1. English language—Textbooks for foreign speakers. 2. English
language—Idioms—Problems, exercises, etc.   I. Title.
PE1128.W367   1995
428.3′4—dc20
                                                    94-321212
                                                        CIP

5 6 7 8 9 10-CRS-009998

To Luke,
for showing me the miracle
of learning English
as a first language;
and Bryn,
who came into being
at the same time as this book.

CONTENTS

Introduction   ix

1   NEGOTIATION   1

black and white/ no ifs, ands, or buts/ rule out/ have it both ways/ up in the air/ pros and cons/ fine line/ not see the forest for the trees/ see something in a whole new light/ right under one's nose/ change one's tune/ make a plug

2   ROMANCE   19

head over heels in love/ stars in one's eyes/ put someone on a pedestal/ feel ten feet tall/ look like a million bucks/ promise the moon/ lay it on thick/ breathing room/ no strings attached/ know where one stands/ get something/someone off one's mind/ give someone a ring

3   PROBLEM SOLVING   37

open a can of worms/ blow it/ in over one's head/ keep a level head/ cut corners/ slip one's mind/ till the cows come home/ throw in the towel/ right around the corner/ cross that bridge when one comes to it/ get something off the ground/ off the top of one's head/ odds are

4   MAKING AN IMPRESSION   55

make a mark/ take center stage/ hands down/ have a corner on something/ strike a chord/ feather in one's cap/ ahead of one's time/ bring to one's feet/ put one's name on the line/ raise eyebrows/ off the beaten path/ warm up to/ hand over fist/ flash in the pan

5   FACING DEFEAT   75

uphill battle/ not have a prayer/ bite off more than one can chew/ slip through one's fingers/ too close for comfort/ sitting duck/ wipe out/ stop something in its tracks/ take it out on someone/ bring to one's knees/ miss the boat/ save face

6   EFFORT   93

put one's best foot forward/ make a splash/ have an edge/ get a leg up on someone/ bend over backwards/ stick one's neck out/ go to great lengths/ go to the ends of the earth/ on the go/ take something in stride/ toe the line/ have a good head on one's shoulders/ let someone down

7   AMBITION   111

corporate ladder/ fast track/ top banana/ call the shots/ take the heat/ keep up with the times/ make something fly/ have a nose for something/ mean business/ feather one's nest/ nest egg/ follow in someone's footsteps/ open doors

8 LEISURE 129

take it easy/ live it up/ have a blast/ paint the town red/ make one's day/ catch one's eye/ take one's breath away/ top-of-the-line/ dressed to kill/ keep up with the Joneses/ beneath one/ at one's feet/ on the house

9 ARGUING 147

make mountains out of molehills/ get a rise out of someone/ drive someone crazy/ cheap shot/ show one's true colors/ mean beans/ take a hike/ four-letter words/ couldn't care less/ cut it out/ give someone a break/ clear the air

10 MONEY 165

doesn't grow on trees/ in the red/ in the black/ stretched too thin/ cost (or charge) an arm and a leg/ take someone to the cleaners/ for a song/ bounce a check/ cough up/ hang on/ live within one's means/ search high and low/ get one's hands on something/ stay put

11 GOSSIP 183

drop in/ stay in touch/ come alive/ keep something bottled up/ floor someone/ make waves/ out of this world/ get the picture/ the last word/ travel in the wrong circles/ fairweather friend/ egg on one's face

12 ACHIEVING SUCCESS 203

get rolling/ get one's gears turning/ learn the ropes/ no sweat/ go by the book/ to the letter/ worth one's salt/ stack up/ snowed under/ give someone the runaround/ middle-of-the-road/ go belly-up

APPENDIXES

Glossary 223

Tapescript and Answer Key 233

Acknowledgments

I would like to thank the students and staff of the English Language Center in Los Angeles for their invaluable comments, advice, and support–particularly as they applied to this project.

I would also like to express my gratitude to all those patient people at Longman who provided much assistance and guidance through the early stages of this manuscript.

My deepest appreciation is reserved for my husband, Peter, who has largely been responsible for keeping the dream of writing this book alive, and who has always been available to help me think of new ideas or to proofread old ones.

INTRODUCTION

TO THE TEACHER

English, as native speakers use it, is largely instinctual and intuitive, peppered with informal and nonstandard expressions and idioms. Those who do not share a native speaker's comfort level in English, even after achieving mastery over the formal elements of the language, often generate speech that may be perfectly understandable, but that lacks some of those expressions that make English come alive. Nonnatives may also be completely bewildered by the idioms they hear or read, due to their infrequent use in the language classroom and the structural inability to define the phrase word-for-word.

Because many idioms are culture-dependent and even culture-specific, they can only be fully integrated into a student's natural speech patterns after extensive exposure to the type of English we use within our culture. In order to recognize idioms and understand the context in which they are used, students should be exposed to real-life language in which idioms are freely incorporated and can be studied in context.

This textbook provides many different opportunities for students to be exposed to idioms contextualized in authentic language and to generate natural, meaningful discourse using those idioms. A wide range of activities and exercises will ensure that students hear, read, and use the idioms in interesting and engaging ways.

One of the most interesting aspects of this book is that students will learn through a series of real magazine and newspaper advertisements that incorporate the idioms taught in each chapter. Print ads have several advantages over other examples of idioms found in the media. There is relatively little text to distract students from the idiom itself; we can immediately focus on the idiom and how it is used to achieve the desired effect in the advertisement. Students will learn to look for and recognize idioms, even if they do not at first fully comprehend their meanings. They will also be exposed to a wonderful source of informal language that is not generally abundant in standard textbooks. In addition, advertising makes valuable allusions to the American experience. While those cultural allusions will almost certainly mean little to a nonnative interpreting the ad by himself or herself, they can provide plenty of grist for discussion of culture and history from a native's point of view. Last but not least, the principal advantage of using ads is that we can find, with relatively little effort, many examples of idioms used in an authentic context in practically any newspaper or magazine we pick up, so you can easily start and maintain a personal classroom collection, either on your own, or with your students' help.

The lessons in the text are structured in such a way as to provide the following advantages. Students will

* practice their understanding of the idioms and how they are used through an array of reading and listening texts, exercises, discussion questions, and open-ended problem-solving situations.

* learn to anticipate and recognize idioms within a natural context.

- be exposed to portrayals of American culture and have opportunities to discuss them.
- identify and discuss examples of irony.
- expand vocabulary by identifying words with more than one meaning.
- identify literal and figurative meanings of words and phrases.
- retain idioms and their meanings longer.

STRUCTURE AND USE OF THE TEXT

The Idiom Advantage has been written with high-intermediate to advanced students in mind. It is composed of twelve chapters, each introducing approximately twelve new idioms. The number of idioms per chapter has been limited in order to facilitate the learning and retention of each idiom. The format of the chapters is the same throughout the text, and the chapters are discrete rather than interdependent, so they can be taught in any order. The basic outline of each chapter and a brief description of each section's objective follows. It is my hope that each teacher that uses this book will feel free to pick and choose the activities and exercises that best fit his or her teaching style or lesson focus. Each chapter incorporates a wide range of highly controlled to open-ended activities, but not all must necessarily be worked into every lesson plan.

I. LEARNING THE IDIOMS

WARMING UP

Various types of questions and activities serve to get the students warmed up and talking about a number of high-interest topics before they begin to learn the idioms. The students are usually instructed to work in groups or to wander about the class, filling out grids or interview sheets as they talk to their classmates.

GETTING TO KNOW THE IDIOMS

A. Listening for Understanding

The students are exposed to the idioms for the first time through this taped passage. A list of questions intended to measure comprehension and the ability to extrapolate is provided for the students to examine before they listen to the tape. Each of the introductory passages has a different format, including (but not limited to) letters, dialogues, a news article, an excerpt from a book, a travel brochure, and a multiple-choice survey. This activity is not intended to be used to focus on the idioms, but rather to promote discussion of the material that forms the larger context for the idioms. At this stage it is not important that students understand the meaning of each idiom, or even that they recognize the idioms when they hear them, as long as they understand the meaning of the passage as a whole.

B. Identifying the Idioms

The students are given the opportunity to read the passage to which they have just listened. They are instructed at this point to underline the idioms and number them on a list in the order in which they find them throughout the passage. They still do not need to understand the exact meaning of each idiom, but they should be thinking about it.

C. Getting the Meaning

Students guess the meanings of the idioms from context in this exercise. It is often helpful to have students work in pairs or small groups on this. Students might also be encouraged to go back to the introductory passage to see how the idiom was used in that context as well. Although there is a complete glossary at the back of the book, it should be used for reference only, rather than as an answer key for this exercise.

PRACTICING THE IDIOMS

D. Choosing the Best Answer

This listening exercise will further help students understand how the idioms are used. Students listen to a series of statements on the tape and choose the best answer in a multiple choice or true-false format. An answer key for this exercise is provided in the back.

E. Retelling the Story

This exercise is optional; it may be used as a homework assignment or for additional practice as time allows. The idioms from the introductory passage have been rephrased here in separate sentences. The students are instructed to determine which idiom from the passage each refers to, and to restate the given sentence by writing a new sentence. The sentences in the exercise are in the same order as the idioms in the introductory passage. An answer key has been provided, but teachers and students should be aware that there is no single correct answer for each; the use of the right idiom in a grammatically correct sentence would make practically any answer correct.

F. Putting the Idioms into Practice

This exercise gives students additional practice using the idioms in a different, slightly more open-ended format. The type of activity varies with each chapter, from fill-in-the-blank exercises to less structured activities, such as writing headlines for newspaper articles. Again, an answer key has been provided, but use with caution: The answers given are not always the only ones possible.

II. IDENTIFYING THE IDIOMS IN ADS

INTERPRETING THE ADS

Most students find it a real challenge to interpret the ads without a solid understanding of the idiom involved. In this section, therefore, each advertisement is accompanied by a list of questions designed to help the students understand the intended message of the advertisers. Students might be assigned to work on the ads in groups to stimulate additional discussion.

THINKING ABOUT THE ADS

This activity deals with other, nonidiomatic aspects of the advertisements. It can be used to promote discussion of culture, values, or advertising techniques, as exemplified by the ads.

III. USING THE IDIOMS

USING THE IDIOMS IN SPEECH

A. One-minute Speech

This activity provides a topic for each individual to develop and then present to the members of his/her group in a short speech.

B. Group Discussion

This second discussion activity presents a different topic to be evaluated and discussed by all the members of the group.

C. Debate

This activity presents two sides of an issue and asks students to take a side and debate it with their partners. If more students favor one side over the other, you may have to assign students to debate a particular side.

D. Role Plays

This activity comprises two role plays suggested for additional practice of idioms in natural conversation. These should be conducted in pairs, as each role play has only two roles described. The students may do both role plays or choose the one they like better. The second one usually has something to do with the topic and characters introduced in the introductory passage.

USING THE IDIOMS IN WRITING

E. Writing with Idioms

This exercise provides additional opportunities to practice the idioms taught. The format changes with each chapter, but instructions to the students always include some kind of written assignment. This exercise might be assigned for homework.

F. Advertising with Idioms

This activity provides an opportunity for students to try their hand at creating an advertisement of their own, using an idiomatic expression.

Some additional features of *The Idiom Advantage* are as follows:

- **Introductory ad:** In keeping with the focal point of this text, a single advertisement is printed at the beginning of each chapter. While the meaning of the idiom may or may not be apparent, this provides an excellent opportunity to discuss in general terms the focus, appeal, and intended audience of the ad. Other advertisements are printed later in the chapter, and at that point, the students will return to the introductory ad and discuss it in more detail.

- **Cassette tape:** The first exercise on the cassette is meant to provide listening practice at the beginning of the chapter with the introductory passage. Students should be instructed to listen for comprehension only. After listening once, however, if you prefer to have students listen for the idioms and check them off the list, that is an option also. The other taped exercise gives students additional practice in discerning the meaning of each idiom in context.

- **Glossary:** A complete glossary appears in the back of the text. The idioms are listed alphabetically, along with their corresponding chapter. In addition to definitions, notes relating to grammar, structure, and pragmatics have been included. Examples are provided for each idiom.

TO THE STUDENT

By now, I'm sure you have come to the conclusion that learning English is a piece of cake, right? Ok, while it may not be easy (*a piece of cake*), it should be fun and interesting. However, without idioms to add spice to the language, it may well be dull and boring. Idioms are what make English come alive. Idioms play an important part in the language of most native speakers, and they are probably the most confusing part of the language you have been exposed to. I hope that the activities and exercises in this book will help you understand and speak English more like a native speaker.

One of the fun and interesting things about this text is that authentic advertisements for products or services sold in the United States are used to illustrate how people sometimes "play" with language. Because many of these ads are difficult to understand without knowing the idioms, you will first learn and practice the idioms in each chapter and then look at the ads and try to explain what they mean. Following the ads, you will have additional opportunities to practice the idioms in discussion and writing activities.

As you learn the idioms in this book, I hope that you will also become increasingly aware of the idioms used in various contexts all around you. Even if you don't always understand exactly what they mean, simply recognizing when and where they are being used is an important first step to understanding. Above all, I hope you will have fun with idioms.

NEGOTIATION

Idioms

BLACK AND WHITE

NO IFS, ANDS, OR BUTS

RULE OUT

HAVE IT BOTH WAYS

UP IN THE AIR

PROS AND CONS

FINE LINE

NOT SEE THE FOREST FOR THE TREES

SEE SOMETHING IN A WHOLE NEW LIGHT

RIGHT UNDER ONE'S NOSE

CHANGE ONE'S TUNE

MAKE A PLUG

I Learning the Idioms

WARMING UP

Complete the following activity and questions in pairs or small groups. Compare answers and discuss with your classmates.

1. Fill in the grid below by listing five different types of crimes (for example, robbery, selling drugs, running a red light). Decide on a punishment for each crime. Then ask two of your classmates what they think the punishment should be for each of those crimes.

Crime	Punishment		
	You	1st Classmate	2nd Classmate

2. Can you think of any act that is against the law in one country but not in another? Do you know of any law in this country that would not apply in your country, or vice versa?

3. Should people who unknowingly commit a crime because they did not understand the law be held responsible for their actions?

4. Can an act be legal but immoral? Can an act be morally right but unlawful? Give examples.

5. Discuss the following situation with your classmates:

Three sailors were adrift on a life raft after their ship had sunk during a storm. After twenty-five days with no food and little water, together they agreed to draw lots to determine which one of the three would be killed and eaten by the other two. Otherwise, they would all die. Although the loser objected strenuously when his lot was drawn, the other two killed and ate him anyway. Later, the two survivors were rescued and taken back to their homeland. Should the two sailors be tried for murder? Why or why not?

GETTING TO KNOW THE IDIOMS

A. Listening for Understanding

Listen to the following article about two immigrants to the United States who were accused of a crime. Consider these questions as you listen to the article. Afterward, discuss the answers with your classmates in pairs or small groups.

1. What crime were the two men accused of? What had they done to be charged with that crime?

2. What two groups held opposing viewpoints of the case? List the arguments used for and against the two men.

3. Do you agree that the men should have been brought to trial? Why or why not? If you had been on the jury, would you have found the men guilty or innocent?

4. If the men had been convicted, how should they have been punished?

5. What would have happened to the two men if they had committed the same act in your country?

B. Identifying the Idioms

Next, read the article to which you have just listened. Throughout this article you will find the idioms listed below. Underline the idioms, and number them on the list in the order in which you find them. Can you tell what they mean by how they are used?

_____ black and white

_____ change one's tune

_____ right under someone's nose

_____ not see the forest for the trees

_____ see something in a whole new light

_____ rule out

_____ no ifs, ands, or buts

_____ fine line

_____ have it both ways

_____ up in the air

_____ make a plug

_____ pros and cons

THE PROS AND CONS OF THE AMERICAN DREAM

Few cases tried in a court of law are absolutely black and white. Although justice may seem to favor one side in the beginning, ultimately there is often a fine line between right and wrong, innocent and guilty, victim and criminal. Take, for example, the case of two Southeast Asian refugees in Los Angeles who were accused of killing their pet dog for food. Were these men guilty of committing a vicious crime against an animal, or were they victims of a foreign culture with which they were not sufficiently familiar?

Most Americans readily eat the meat of various animals—cows, chickens, pigs, even cute little ones like ducks and rabbits—but certainly not of dogs or cats; and because many Americans feel so strongly about their pets, there are laws protecting the animals from negligence and abuse. Where the two men came from, however, dogs were routinely turned into dinner, and the refugees did not know they would be offending American sensibilities by eating their dog. In fact, they killed the animal right under the nose of their American neighbor, who, to their surprise, immediately called the police. The two men were charged with cruelty to animals.

Animal rights activists, who for years have loudly proclaimed that animals also deserve protection under the law, were outraged over the act. Using the trial to make a plug for their cause, they picketed the court proceedings, demanding that the "evil criminals" pay heavily for what they had done. They even sent death threats to the two men. Their position was clear: The men should be severely punished or expelled from the country, no ifs, ands, or buts about it.

Others, more inclined to measure the weight of the crime against the trauma that the refugees were undergoing, tried to focus on some of the cultural issues involved. They pointed out that those who were obsessed with the dog's death could not see the forest for the trees; in their passion for revenge, the dog's defenders could not recognize the broader cultural issues of this case. If Americans were less ethnocentric, it was said, they might see the refugees' "crime" in a whole new light. In fact, they might begin to understand that their American cultural values were not necessarily defined by universal moral truths. And if those self-righteous Americans ever lived in another country and had to abide strictly by that country's cultural standards, they might change their tune completely.

While both sides argued vigorously against each other in the media, the case presented by the lawyers for the prosecution and the defense would ultimately decide the fate of the two men.

The defense attorney first established that because his clients could not have known they were doing anything wrong, any intent to deliberately break the law must be ruled out. But he also argued that the charge of cruelty to animals would only apply if the men had tortured the dog before killing it. After all, he said, we kill animals every day to eat them, and no one would suggest that a steak dinner resulted from cruelty to animals!

On the other hand, the prosecutor claimed that immigrants should be held responsible for understanding and obeying the laws of the land in which they live. Otherwise, there could be no uniform standard of justice for the country, and chaos would ensue. Although he acknowl-

edged the cultural differences in their background, he said the men could not have it both ways; if they broke the law, they should be punished, regardless of their country of origin.

Were the two refugees innocent or guilty? The outcome of the trial was up in the air while the jury deliberated. They carefully considered the pros and cons of each side and the implications of convicting the bewildered men of their crime or of letting them go. Finally, they rendered the verdict: The two men were found not guilty.

C. Getting the Meaning

Notice the highlighted phrase in each of the following statements. Pay attention to how the idiom is used, and try to guess its meaning. You may also refer to the preceding article. Write the meaning of the idiom on the line. The first one is done for you.

1. I've tried to convince John that our financial status is not **black and white**—just because we're not rich, it doesn't mean we're poor.

   <u>Two sides that are extremes: right or wrong, or good or bad, with nothing</u>
   <u>in between</u>

2. Make sure he is the right person for you before you marry him; there is a **fine line** between infatuation and true love.

   _____

3. I can't believe she spent most of the day reading magazines **right under her boss's nose!**

_____

4. The president appeared at a rally in Washington to **make a plug** for his new economic plan.

_____

5. The final deadline for the project is February 10. You must complete it by then, **no ifs, ands, or buts.**

_____

6. Mr. Kramer **can't see the forest for the trees.** He is more concerned about his students' handwriting than the content of their papers.

_____

7. After his girlfriend broke up with him, Danny recognized that he had not been sensitive to her needs. He began to **see** their relationship **in a whole new light.**

_____

8. You may think it's Brad's fault that he can't find a job, but if you suddenly lost your job, you might **change your tune.**

_____

9. Unfortunately, I think we must **rule out** a trip to the beach this weekend. The weather forecast is for rain.

_____

10. You can't **have it both ways.** If you want to get rich, you'll have to go to work; you can't just spend your days at the beach.

_____

11. The future of the health care center is still **up in the air**; we cannot make any firm plans until funding has been secured.

_____

12. The death penalty is not legal in every state; the **pros and cons** of capital punishment continue to be argued vigorously in legislatures around the country.

_____

PRACTICING THE IDIOMS

D. Choosing the Best Answer

Listen carefully to the following taped statements. Read the choices listed below for each statement you hear. Select the sentence that best relates to the original statement, and circle the corresponding letter.

1. a. She changed her tune in the movie.
    b. She wanted to make a plug for the movie.
    c. She thought the movie was black and white.

2. a. You can't have it both ways.
    b. You can't see the forest for the trees.
    c. You can't rule marriage out.

3. a. They are protesting that the school's grading policy is too black and white.
    b. They are angry that the teachers changed their tune.
    c. They understand the pros and cons of the new grading policy.

4. a. He couldn't see the forest for the trees.
    b. He ruled out firing his secretary.
    c. He wanted to have it both ways.

5. a. They saw the painting in a whole new light.
    b. It was right under his nose!
    c. The painting is still up in the air!

6. a. Susie's clothes are very fashionable—no ifs, ands, or buts about it.
    b. Fashion has many pros and cons.
    c. There is often a fine line between high fashion and bad taste.

7. a. I guess that rules him out.
    b. Maybe he can make a plug for the job.
    c. I think George will change his tune.

8. a. She feels the contract is right under her nose.
    b. She wants to discuss the pros and cons of her contract.
    c. There are no ifs, ands, or buts about it.

9. a. I can't see the forest for the trees.
    b. It's still up in the air.
    c. I see things in a whole new light.

10. a. Doctors are likely to rule out nationalized health care.
    b. Doctors want to have it both ways.
    c. Doctors often discuss the pros and cons of nationalized health care.

11. a. She realized he was right under her nose.
     b. I guess she changed her tune.
     c. She felt their relationship was up in the air.

12. a. There's a fine line between winning and losing.
     b. There are no ifs, ands, or buts about the game.
     c. The game is still up in the air.

E. Retelling the Story—Optional Activity

Read the article on pages 4–5 again. The sentences below refer to statements in that article. On the lines below, restate the sentences, using the appropriate idiom. The first one is done for you.

1. There are many cases that come to trial that are not easily decided; rarely is one side all good or all bad.

    Not all cases that are tried in a court of law are black and white.

2. It is sometimes difficult to determine who is truly at fault; there is often a subtle distinction between the innocent and guilty parties in a case.

    _____

3. The men killed the dog in plain view of their neighbor, who then notified the authorities.

    _____

4. Animal rights activists used the trial to publicize the objectives of their organization.

    _____

5. Their critics stated plainly that the men should either be punished or forced to leave the country, with no other options considered.

    _____

6. Some of the men's sympathizers accused the activists of being so consumed with the details of the dog's death that they were unable to recognize the larger issues.

    _____

7. They said that if some Americans were not so convinced of their moral superiority, they might view the case from a totally different perspective.

    _____

8. They even suggested that the experience of living in a foreign country would cause many Americans to have a completely different opinion of the case.

    _____

9. The defense lawyer claimed that because the two men hadn't known that killing their dog was wrong, the possibility that they broke the law on purpose must be eliminated.

_____

10. The prosecutor said that the men could not benefit from living in the United States without also accepting responsibility for obeying its laws.

_____

11. The verdict in the trial was uncertain while the jury discussed the case.

_____

12. The members of the jury argued about the advantages and disadvantages of each side of the case.

_____

F. Putting the Idioms into Practice

Part I

Francine Lewis and Scott Darby are running for mayor in the upcoming election. Their positions on three key issues are summarized below.

FRANCINE LEWIS

transportation: Although the budget is very limited, she supports investment in both railways and highways.

education: She wants a special panel of experts to discuss the advantages and disadvantages of private management of the school system before she decides on her position.

health care: Since Ms. Lewis used to be a nurse, she often uses her speaking opportunities to publicize the need for more and better-trained nurses.

SCOTT DARBY

transportation: Because of limited funds, he believes that all the money should go to highway construction, and that railways should be eliminated.

education: He says the government can do the best job of managing schools for less money, and he refuses to discuss it further.

health care: He once said that all medical fees and expenses should be set by a government agency, but when a group of doctors contributed generously to his campaign fund, he changed his position on the matter.

As the candidates campaign against each other, they try to discredit their opponent. Using the idioms listed below, write how Ms. Lewis would characterize Mr. Darby's positions on each of the issues, and vice versa. Use each idiom only once. Both of their speeches have been started for you.

pros and cons   **make a plug**
no ifs, ands, or buts **rule out**
change one's tune   **have it both ways**

FRANCINE LEWIS: "Scott Darby would ruin this beautiful city! Just look at what he plans to do to transportation! Of course highway construction is important, but he would **rule out** any spending on railways! _____

_____

_____

_____

_____

_____

_____

_____

_____

_____

                                                            "

SCOTT DARBY: "Francine Lewis must think that the government has an unlimited source of money. We simply cannot afford to build highways *and* railways, but she wants to_____

_____

_____

_____

_____

_____

_____

_____

_____

_____

                                                            "

Part II

Brett Martin recently opened a convenience store and hired Lisa Henderson to work as a part-time clerk. He had known Lisa for many years and believed that she would be an honest and hard-working employee. However, a few weeks after she started working, a customer saw her take twenty dollars from the cash register and put it in her pocket. The customer told Mr. Martin, and he immediately called Lisa into his office. Complete the conversation between Lisa and her boss. Fill in the blanks with the idioms listed below.

black and white
up in the air
fine line

can't see the forest for the trees
see things in a whole new light
right under the nose

BRETT: Honesty is a _____ issue. You cannot be halfway
 honest. You stole twenty dollars from me _____ of a
 customer! How could you do that?

LISA: I wasn't stealing; I just needed to borrow some money to buy lunch. I was
 planning on paying it back!

BRETT: There's a _____ between borrowing and stealing. I
 thought I could trust you, but I'm starting to _____ .

LISA: Brett, maybe you're so worried about this one incident that you
 _____ . You know I've been an excellent employee
 —I'm always on time, courteous, efficient, and hardworking. Why, just last
 week you promised me a raise!

BRETT: Well, right now that raise is _____ . I'll have to
 think about it. But first, give me back the money.

LISA: Oh, sure, here it is. By the way, Brett, will you lend me twenty bucks?

II Finding the Idioms in Ads

INTERPRETING THE ADS

Look at the following advertisements. First determine what is being advertised and what idiom is featured in the ad. Review the meaning of the idiom. Then answer the questions corresponding to each ad.

1. How many times can you find the word *light* in this ad? Does it always mean the same thing? What are the different meanings of *light* ?

2. Many Americans are preoccupied with "healthy" foods. What about this ad might appeal to health-conscious consumers?

3. Why does the ad claim that "Wesson puts olive oil in a whole new light"?

4. The woman shown in this ad is the actress Florence Henderson. Can you guess what type of TV role she is most famous for? Does it matter who she is?

1. What does the picture show?

2. How does the picture relate to the idiom?

3. Is this company advertising a truck with a cab at both ends?

4. If this truck runs only on gasoline, which it does, in what way can consumers "have it both ways"?

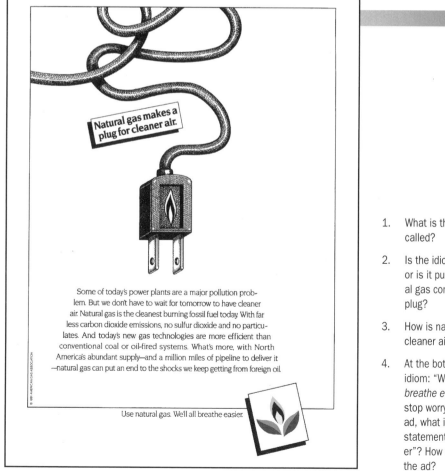

1. What is the item pictured in this ad called?

2. Is the idiom used in a literal sense, or is it purely idiomatic? Could natural gas come through an electrical plug?

3. How is natural gas responsible for cleaner air?

4. At the bottom of the ad is another idiom: "We'll all breathe easier." To *breathe easier* means to relax and stop worrying. As it is used in this ad, what is another meaning of the statement, "We'll all breathe easier"? How does it relate to the rest of the ad?

1. What is the idiomatic meaning of "your future is up in the air"? What is the literal meaning?

2. At the bottom of the ad, it says, "So whatever your dreams are, if you want to get them off the ground, call. . . ." What do you think it means to *get something off the ground*? How does that idiom fit into the theme of the ad?

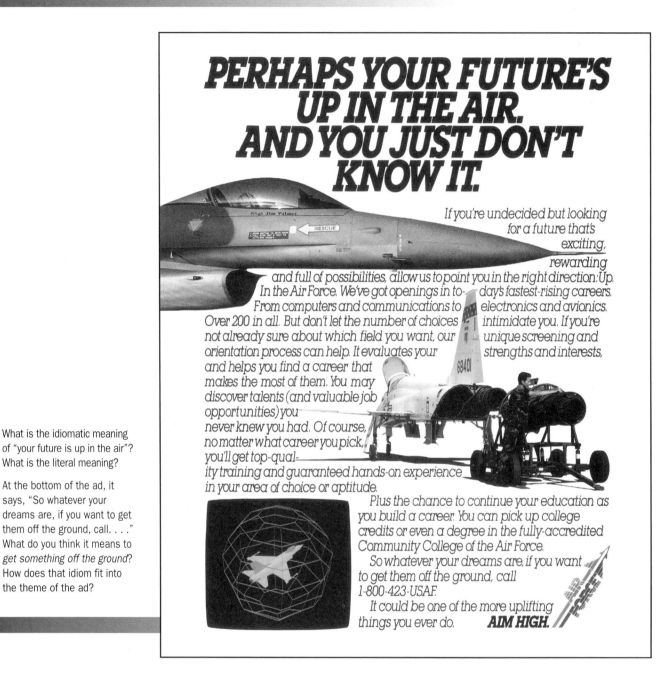

1. What is the message AT&T is trying to give consumers?

2. The idiom is printed in very large, bold type. How does that support the meaning of the idiom?

3. What claims does AT&T make to prove they are "the best in the business"?

4. Do you think this ad is effective in delivering its message? Why?

THINKING ABOUT THE ADS

Review the ads from this chapter. Based on the messages contained in the ads, choose the one that you think best illustrates American cultural values. Complete statements one through four based on that ad.

1. This ad would appeal to an American audience because . . . .

2. It is important to many Americans to . . . .

3. Other examples in American life that show how Americans feel about this issue or value are . . . .

4. This ad would/would not appeal to an audience from my country because . . . .

5. The ad that I liked the best is . . . .

6. The ad that made the best use of an idiom is . . . because . . . .

III Using the Idioms

USING THE IDIOMS IN SPEECH

A. One-minute Speech

Write a brief outline before presenting your one-minute speech to your classmates. Be sure to use the idioms from this chapter in your speech.

In some African countries, elephants are near extinction because they are hunted and killed for their ivory tusks, which are then sold for a marginal profit on the black market. Beyond the tragedy of greatly diminished numbers of animals, the poachers are only hurting themselves and their African brothers and sisters. As the animals become more and more scarce, so does the hunters' potential for any further income. Furthermore, since African tourism and safaris create greater economic opportunities than selling ivory, it would be much more advantageous for the Africans to encourage protection for the elephant herds, rather than their destruction. You have been assigned to speak to a group of African tribesmen to try to convince them to help stop the killing of elephants in their homeland. Tell the tribesmen that it is for *their* benefit that the elephants should no longer be hunted.

B. Group Discussion

Participate in the following discussion, using the idioms from this chapter.

Your friend is in her second year at college and is trying to decide what to choose as her major course of study. She wants to be a writer, and in fact has already won several awards for her poetry. Her parents would like her to become a teacher so that she at least will have a steady income after graduation.

Discuss the following with your group, and remember to use the idioms from this chapter in your discussion.

- your friend's position

- her parents' position

- the advantages and disadvantages of writing full time

- how her parents might feel if she signed a lucrative contract with a major publishing company

- what, if anything, she could do to please her parents as well as herself

- what you think she should do

C. Debate: School for Pay

Read the situation and choose to defend either side of the following question: Should some students get paid for attending school? *Before you begin, jot down the arguments supporting your position. Remember to use as many of the idioms from this chapter as you can.*

East Hills High School is similar to many other high schools around the country. Although most students complete their education, many drop out before they graduate. Because of this problem, an innovative program at East Hills was designed to keep students in school. At-risk students—those who have previously had trouble staying in school—are paid five dollars for every day they attend all their classes on time, do all their homework, and come prepared to class. The program seems to be effective for those students it has targeted, but there has been a protest launched by the students who have never had problems and therefore don't get paid.

D. Role Plays

Imagine yourself in one of the situations described below. Act it out with another member of your class, using as many idioms from this chapter as you can in your conversation. You and your partner may want to write a brief script of the role play before acting it out.

1. (priest, prisoner)

PRIEST: You believe that everyone should have a chance to change his or her life, even convicted criminals. You talk to prisoners every day, asking if they want to confess their sins, and encouraging them to repent.

PRISONER: Before you were in prison, you didn't care about anyone but yourself. Now that you've had some time to think about all the people you've hurt, you feel very bad, and you see things from a different perspective.

2. (defense attorney, prosecutor. Review the article on pages 4–5 to help you build your case.)

DEFENSE ATTORNEY: You are defending two Southeast Asian clients who have been charged with cruelty to animals for killing their dog for food. Construct your case carefully, and convince the jury that they are innocent.

PROSECUTOR: You believe that the two men who killed their dog to eat it are guilty of cruelty to animals. Even though they are not native Americans, they should be bound by the same laws as everyone else. You must convince the jury of this.

USING THE IDIOMS IN WRITING

E. Writing with Idioms

The following story is only half-written. Read it carefully, and decide how it ends. Then finish writing the story, using the idioms from this chapter.

Shortly after her father died, Nadine suggested to her husband, Randall, that they invite her mother to live with them. Although they didn't have a lot of room, Randall willingly agreed, and soon Nadine's mother moved in. It wasn't long before Randall regretted the invitation; his mother-in-law was making life absolutely miserable for him. He didn't even want to come home after work because he hated her constant complaining and their total lack of privacy. However, Randall realized that Nadine felt much better knowing that her mother was not alone. Nadine also appreciated her mother's help around the house and with the children. Randall didn't know what to do, but he decided that he must speak to Nadine about the problem before another day went by. . . .

F. Advertising with Idioms

Make up an advertisement for any type of product not *advertised in the ads in this chapter, using one or more of the idioms you have just learned. Follow the steps listed below.*

1. Choose a product or service that you would like to advertise.

2. Determine your *audience*—the people most likely to buy your product or service.

3. Determine what value(s) would appeal to that audience. How are you going to incorporate that value into your ad?

4. Make up a slogan, using one of the idioms from this chapter.

5. Decide what visual cues (pictures, etc.) will accompany the slogan.

6. Write the rest of the ad.

7. Present it to the class. Do you think this ad would appeal to the other members of your class?

Thurs. 9/30/10

Idioms

HEAD OVER HEELS IN LOVE

STARS IN ONE'S EYES

PUT SOMEONE ON A PEDESTAL

FEEL TEN FEET TALL

LOOK LIKE A MILLION BUCKS

PROMISE THE MOON

LAY IT ON THICK

BREATHING ROOM

NO STRINGS ATTACHED

KNOW WHERE ONE STANDS

GET SOMEONE OFF ONE'S MIND

GIVE SOMEONE A RING

HEAD OVER HEELS.
THE DIAMONDS OF TIFFANY.

TIFFANY & CO.

NEW YORK BEVERLY HILLS SAN FRANCISCO SOUTH COAST PLAZA SAN DIEGO DALLAS HOUSTON PALM BEACH WASHINGTON, D.C.
CHICAGO TROY ATLANTA BOSTON PHILADELPHIA TORONTO TO INQUIRE. 800-526-0649

I Learning the Idioms

WARMING UP

In small groups of only men and only women, discuss the following questions. Then compare the men's responses to the women's. How are they similar? How are they different? What accounts for those similarities or differences?

1. How accurate are your first impressions of the people you meet? Do you find that you often change your opinion of a person after knowing him/her for some time? Do your later impressions usually change for the better or for the worse? Do you think men or women have more accurate first impressions of the people they meet?

2. What are the first things that you notice when you meet someone of the opposite sex? Make a list of five items, and rank them in order of importance.

3. Which of those items on your list do you think would continue to be important to you in a long-term relationship?

4. Do you believe in "love at first sight"? Explain.

5. Agree or disagree with the following statements:

   • Women have a fundamental need to feel dependent on men.

   • Women are attracted to men who take a dominant role in the relationship.

   • Women are more emotional than men.

   • Men are more rational than women.

   • It is better to be single than to be married.

6. Discuss the following situation with your group.

   Chantal and Hans met in English class and began spending time together. At first, they were just helping each other study, but soon they became romantically involved. Hans is falling in love with Chantal. Chantal isn't sure how she feels about Hans because she left her boyfriend, Antoine, to come to study in the United States. Last night, Antoine called and told her that he would be coming to visit her in two days. Hans doesn't know anything about Antoine. Tonight Chantal is having dinner with Hans. What should she do?

GETTING TO KNOW THE IDIOMS

A. Listening for Understanding

Listen to the following two letters, written by a man and woman who just met each other. They are asking two of their friends for advice on how to deal with their relationship. Consider these questions as you listen to the letters. Afterward, discuss the answers with your classmates in pairs or small groups.

1. What happened the evening that John and Tina met? Describe how you think the evening went from the moment they saw each other to when they said good-bye.

2. Can you imagine this kind of an encounter happening in your native country?

3. How does John feel about Tina? How does Tina feel about John?

4. If you were Ted, what advice would you give John? If you were Lori, what advice would you give Tina?

5. Do you think that John and Tina will become romantically involved? Why or why not?

Mon. 10/4/10
#7

B. Identifying the Idioms

Next, read the letters to which you have just listened. Throughout these letters you will find the idioms listed below. Underline the idioms, and number them on the list in the order in which you find them. Can you tell what they mean by how they are used?

_____ **look like a million bucks**   _____ **breathing room**

_____ **feel ten feet tall**   _____ **lay it on thick**

_____ **head over heels in love**   _____ **know where one stands**

_____ **promise (someone) the moon**   _____ **no strings attached**

_____ **stars in one's eyes**   _____ **give someone a ring**

_____ **put someone on a pedestal**   _____ **get someone/something off one's mind**

HEAD OVER HEELS

Dear Ted,

I wish you were here, instead of a thousand miles away. I've really got to talk to you! You know me better than anybody, so what I have to say may shock you. Ted, I'm head over heels in love with a girl I only met last night. It may seem crazy, but I don't even want to see anyone else. You may think it's a little early to make such an important decision, but I'm telling you, this is it! I know it sounds like I've got stars in my eyes, but you would understand if you saw her. I just can't get her off my mind. As soon as I saw her walk into the party, I knew she was something special. She looked like a million bucks—long black hair, big grey eyes, wearing a fabulous green dress—I knew I had to meet her. We spent most of the evening together, and then she came over to my place after the party and we talked for hours. She made me feel ten feet tall—I can't remember ever feeling so happy. Finally she said she had to go. I wanted to ask her to stay with me forever, but I need to make sure she feels the same way. I've got to know where I stand! I know I can't promise her the moon, but I would give her my best. So what do you think? Ted, write soon. This is serious, and I need your advice.

Your buddy,

John

Dear Lori,

    I tried calling you this morning, but your line was busy, so I thought I'd write you a note instead. We need to talk! I hope you're not working late today, because I'm counting on you to give me some good advice.

    Remember that guy I left the party with last night? His name is John. He's very nice, and I think he really likes me. I guess there's nothing wrong with that, but he barely knows me, and I hate it when guys put me on a pedestal. It's so much harder to have a normal relationship with someone who thinks you're perfect —don't you agree? Anyway, he got serious pretty fast last night, and we had only just met! He told me that I was just right for him, and that he'd never been with anyone so beautiful, and we'd make a wonderful couple, and on and on. He was really laying it on thick. It's all very nice to hear, but I'm just not ready to get involved with anyone right now. I need some breathing room, you know? I'd like to take it slow—maybe go out with him now and then, with no strings attached. He promised he'd call me today, and I don't know what to tell him. So, what do you think? Give me a ring as soon as you get home!

    See you,

Tina

C. Getting the Meaning

Notice the highlighted phrase in each of the following statements. Pay attention to how the idiom is used, and try to guess its meaning. You may also refer to the preceding letters. Write the meaning of the idiom on the line. The first one is done for you.

1. The story of Romeo and Juliet is so romantic! Imagine being **head over heels** in love like they were!

      very much in love

2. When Ben and Maggie talk about each other, they have **stars in their eyes**. You can tell they just got married.

   _____

3. When I visited Linda in the hospital last week, I saw a little boy who was seriously ill. He had such a sad look on his face. Since then, I haven't been able to **get him off my mind**.

   _____

Tues. 10/5/10 #82

4. Tom bought a new gray pinstripe suit and an expensive Italian silk tie for his job interview. He **looked like a million bucks**!

_____

5. Jeannie studied all night for her geography test. When the grades were posted, she **felt ten feet tall**. She was the only one to get 100 percent.

_____

6. Clyde keeps telling me that he just wants to be my friend, but when I make a date with another guy, he gets really jealous. I don't understand; I've got to find out **where I stand** with him.

_____

7. Henry Stone made millions of dollars by telling people that they would become very rich if they invested in his company. He **promised them the moon**, but nobody else made a penny.

_____

8. It's hard to believe that Michael Jackson is a person just like everyone else. Because he is so famous, he has **been put on a pedestal** his whole life.

_____

9. Marlee has sold more encyclopedias than anyone. First, she **lays it on thick** by telling her customers how intelligent and sophisticated they are. After that, they are all willing to buy anything from her.

_____

10. Sadie is having a difficult time at work. Her boss controls practically every movement she makes. If he doesn't give her some **breathing room**, I think she'll quit her job.

_____

11. Lee has already been divorced, so she's not anxious to get married again. Even though she sees Joe quite often, she says there are **no strings attached**.

_____

12. I'm sorry my line was busy last night. Why don't you **give me a ring** this evening, and we can talk then.

_____

PRACTICING THE IDIOMS

D. Choosing the Best Answer

Listen carefully to the following taped statements. Decide if the sentence that corresponds to each is true or false. Circle T if it is true and F if it is false.

1. T /(F) Doug married the woman he loves.
2. (T)/ F Marty probably wanted to see Ken again.
3. (T)/ F I have been singing that song over and over again in my mind.
4. T /(F) Sergeant Gibbs is probably very wealthy.
5. T /(F) Only tall women win the Miss America pageant.
6. T /(F) Kurt doesn't know where his girlfriend is.
7. (T)/ F Dr. Carter isn't able to guarantee a cure for cancer yet.
8. (T)/ F Police officers are expected to be more honest than other people.
9. T /(F) Stewart didn't care what she thought of him.
10. (T)/ F Lena thinks her parents are too strict with her.
11. T /(F) The car is usually tied down with strings to prevent theft.
12. T /(F) Darryl wasn't sure whether or not he should give his girlfriend her wedding ring.

E. Retelling the Story—Optional Activity

Read the letters on pages 22–23 again. The sentences below refer to statements in those letters. On the lines below, restate the sentences, using the appropriate idiom. The first one is done for you.

1. John was deeply in love with Tina, even though they had only just met.

   John was head over heels in love with Tina, even though they had only just met.

2. John was totally infatuated with Tina.

   From the moment he saw her John had stars in his eyes.

3. He couldn't stop thinking about her.

4. Tina looked great! She was beautiful and dressed very attractively.

   _____

5. Tina made John feel wonderful when he was with her.

   _____

6. John wanted to know how Tina felt about him.

   _____

7. He knew that he couldn't guarantee that everything in their future would be perfect, but he would try.

   _____

8. Tina felt that John wasn't treating her like a normal person; it was as if she were perfect.

   _____

9. John spent the evening telling Tina how beautiful she was and how great everything would be if they were together.

   _____

10. Tina needed to feel a sense of independence. She didn't want to be with one person all the time.

    _____

11. She wanted an open relationship, in which she was not bound by any commitments or promises about the future.

    _____

12. Tina wanted Lori to call her on the phone when she got home.

    _____

F. Putting the Idioms into Practice

Natalie and Jake are two characters on the popular soap opera, "Nights of Our Lives ." They are rehearsing a scene for the next show, but they keep forgetting their lines. Complete the dialogue with sentences. Remember to change the idioms as needed to fit the sentences.

NATALIE: Oh, darling, I can't go on like this any longer. One day you say you love me, and the

next day you don't. _____ .
                                                  1. know where one stands

JAKE: Natalie, you're a beautiful woman and you take great care of yourself.

_____ . You're intelligent and charming and talented.
         2. look like a million bucks
Most men would die for your love. But . . .

NATALIE: Stop it! _____ . Say what you really mean!
                    3. lay it on thick

JAKE: I just don't know what I want right now. Maybe I should get away and be by myself for

a while _____ .
                            4. breathing room

NATALIE: Oh, Jake, please don't leave me! I don't know what I would do without you. If you were

gone, I'd go crazy! _____ .
                       5. get someone off one's mind

JAKE: Natalie, please calm down. I'm not the man you think I am.

_____ . You could easily find someone much
         6. put someone on a pedestal
better for you than I am.

NATALIE: No, no, no! Don't do this to me, Jake! You know I can't live without you! When we're

together, _____ . And it wasn't so long ago that you
               7. feel ten feet tall
felt the same way. _____ .
               8. stars in one's eyes

JAKE: You're right. When I first met you, things were great. We were younger then, and more

innocent. _____ . But everything has changed.
            9. head over heels in love
Our relationship is very different now.

NATALIE: Jake, can't we try again? _____ .
                                10. with no strings attached

JAKE: I don't know, Natalie. _____ . I need time to think.
                          11. promise someone the moon

NATALIE: OK, Jake, but don't be gone too long. I'll be waiting to hear from you.

_____ .
                12. give someone a ring

II Finding the Idioms in Ads

INTERPRETING THE ADS

Look at the following advertisements. First determine what is being advertised and what idiom is featured in the ad. Review the meaning of the idiom. Then answer the questions corresponding to each ad.

1. This ad does not have a lot of text. The picture is a significant part of the ad. What is the message of this ad?

2. Who is the principal audience for this ad, men or women? Why?

1. How has Toyota changed the idiom? Why did they do that?

2. According to the picture and the ad text, what will this truck do?

3. Does the original idiom—*to feel ten feet tall* — apply in this ad?

4. There are two other idioms in the text of this ad: "to make the grade," and "to call someone's bluff." Can you find these expressions in the ad? Can you tell what they mean?

4X4

"NOW I KNOW WHAT IT'S LIKE TO FEEL 10,778 FEET TALL."

The 1991 Toyota 4x4 Deluxe V6 is one truck that's not afraid of heights. Its gutsy 3.0-liter electronic fuel-injected V6 pumps out 150 horses and enough torque (180 ft-lbs.) to help you make the grade and then some. No wonder it's the number-one-selling compact 4x4, import or domestic, 10 years running.* With Toyota's legendary reliability you've got what it takes to call anyone's bluff—even on Mt. Rose at 10,778 feet. Call 1-800-GO-TOYOTA for a truck brochure and the location of your nearest dealer.

"I love what you do for me."

🚗 **TOYOTA**

TOYOTA REMINDS YOU TO
TREAD LIGHTLY!
ON PUBLIC AND PRIVATE LAND

Light bar does not provide crash protection.
*Source: R.L. Polk Registration, 1980-1989.
© 1990 Toyota Motor Sales, U.S.A., Inc.

1. How does the picture relate to the ad slogan?

2. What kinds of activities is this truck best suited for? In what way does Toyota "promise you the moon"?

3. Is the statement, "Go ahead, promise them the moon" idiomatic, literal, or both?

WE'RE LAYING IT ON THICK.

We're laying it on thin, too. In fact, we can laminate in plastic from 5 mm to 60 mm thickness.
So call us. We'll stick with you through thick or thin.

Lamination Concepts
612-427-4306

1. *Lamination* is the thin plastic that surrounds and seals paper items that you want to protect and preserve. What kinds of things are laminated?

2. Do you have an ID card or driver's license that is laminated?

3. Which do you think is better—thick or thin lamination? Why?

4. There is a common saying used in this ad: "We'll stick with you through thick or thin." What do you think that means? Is there an equivalent of this saying in your language?

Give Your Family Some Breathing Room.

Give them the remarkably pollution-free air of an Enviracaire system. Enviracaire is the first portable, affordable air cleaner that has taken advanced HEPA filter technology from the laboratory clean room to your living room.

Enviracaire clears the air of 99.97% of impurities from dust, pollen and mold spores to smoke, bacteria, and viruses. And now you can choose from three Enviracaire models.

Give your family truly clean breathing room. Call us now for the Enviracaire dealer near you. 1-800-332-1110.

enviracaire®

Cleaner air means better health.

1. What would the statement "Give your family some breathing room" mean if it were not associated with this product?

2. What does Enviracaire do?

3. What is the literal meaning of the statement "Give your family some breathing room" as it is used in this ad?

1. What does the picture show?

2. Who usually stands at the altar in a church?

3. Is a priest or minister typically male or female?

4. Would you be suprised to see a female minister?

5. How does the Episcopal Church feel about female ministers?

6. This ad has a double meaning. Can you explain the literal, as well as the idiomatic meaning of this ad?

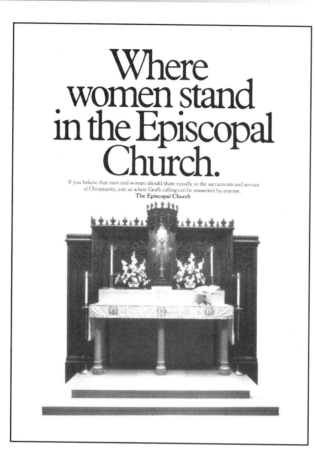

THINKING ABOUT THE ADS

Review the ads from this chapter. Based on the messages contained in the ads, choose the one that you think best illustrates American cultural values. Complete statements one through four based on that ad.

1. This ad would appeal to an American audience because . . . .

2. It is important to many Americans to . . . .

3. Other examples in American life that show how Americans feel about this issue or value are . . . .

4. This ad would/would not appeal to an audience from my country because . . . .

5. The ad that I liked the best is . . . .

6. The ad that made the best use of an idiom is . . . because . . . .

III Using the Idioms

USING THE IDIOMS IN SPEECH

A. One-minute Speech

Write a brief outline before presenting your one-minute speech to your classmates. Be sure to use the idioms from this chapter in your speech.

You may choose to agree or disagree with the following statement:

"Women generally fall in love faster than men and are more committed to a relationship."

Defend your view, explaining why you agree or disagree.

B. Group Discussion

In small groups of only men and only women, complete the following love letter by finishing the sentences that have been started for you. Not every sentence must include an idiom from this chapter, but be sure to use one wherever possible. Before you get started, decide together whose name you would like to write in the first blank.

Dearest _____,

The first time I saw you, _____

When you look at me, _____

You make me _____

I know that I will always _____

Every time I think of you _____

When I'm with you, _____

Would you please _____

     Love always,

_____

C. Debate: Incompatible Marriage Partners?

Read the situation and choose to defend either side of the following question: Should the couple be allowed to marry? *Before you begin, jot down the arguments supporting your position. Remember to use as many of the idioms from this chapter as you can.*

Recently, there was a story in the news about a twenty-three-year-old mentally retarded man who fell in love with a forty-seven-year-old woman. The woman had been married previously and divorced, and was reportedly an alcoholic. The young man's family believed that the woman would take unfair advantage of their son, who had the mental capability of a twelve-year-old. They believed that the pair should not be allowed to marry. The woman claimed that they could help one another and that no one should stand in the way of their love.

D. Role Plays

Imagine yourself in one of the situations described below. Act it out with another member of your class, using as many idioms from this chapter as you can in your conversation. You and your partner may want to write a brief script of the role play before acting it out.

1. (two friends)

FRIEND A: For several months, you have been infatuated with someone who has never paid much attention to you. Finally, in hopes of making this person notice you, you dyed your hair, had plastic surgery, and started wearing wild new clothes. In spite of your new look, he/she still is not interested. You suspect there is someone else in the person's life. You are meeting an old friend today for the first time in over a year.

FRIEND B: You are getting together with a friend whom you haven't seen in a long time. The first thing you notice is that your friend looks and acts like a completely different person. Your friend looks fabulous, but you can tell that he/she still isn't happy. As your friend talks, you realize that the person he/she is interested in is *your* boy/girlfriend! Oh, no! What are you going to say to your friend?

2. (John and Tina)

JOHN: You called Tina earlier today to make a date for dinner this evening. (It is the day after you met.) She sounded kind of funny on the phone, but maybe she was just nervous. So are you. You have decided to ask her to marry you.

TINA: You are going out to dinner with John, and you aren't sure what to tell him. You would like to get to know him better, but you want him to slow down! You have your future all planned: college, a career, travel, and so on, and you are definitely not ready to settle down with one person!

USING THE IDIOMS IN WRITING

E. Writing with Idioms

Part I

Commonly, people who need help resolving personal issues and dilemmas can write to a newspaper or magazine columnist for advice. Answers to these letters are then printed in the newspaper or magazine for everyone to read. Described below are various problems that you want the popular columnist Sally Sue to respond to. Choose one problem, and write a letter to Sally Sue in which you tell about your situation, using the idioms from this chapter.

1. You have a friend who is about to be married to a man she has known for only a month. You don't like this man, and you think that he is only marrying her for her money. Your friend admits that her boyfriend has already "borrowed" huge amounts of money, but she believes that he will pay her back after they are married. Your friend seems to be very much in love with this man and thinks he is perfect for her, even though he treats her badly, spends *her* money, and constantly flirts with other women.

2. You recently met a woman at a business convention who is beautiful, smart, and funny—in short, everything you've always wanted. After going out for several weeks, however, you found out that she had previously been seeing one of your friends. Your friend has been heartbroken since she broke up with him, and you know that he would be very upset to know that you are now dating her. You don't know what to do.

3. You were married for two years to a very jealous man/woman who suspected you of having an affair every time you left the house. Now that you are divorced, however, your ex-husband/ex-wife continues to call you every day and comes to your office and home all the time. Your former spouse has already ruined one relationship, and you are worried about having another for fear that your "ex" will ruin it as well.

Part II

After you have finished, exchange your letter(s) with other members of your class. Discuss solutions to the problem, and then write a letter in response from Sally Sue. Give that letter to the person who originally wrote about the problem.

F. Advertising with Idioms

Make up an advertisement for any type of product not *advertised in the ads in this chapter, using one or more of the idioms you have just learned. Follow the steps listed below.*

1. Choose a product or service that you would like to advertise.

2. Determine your *audience*—the people most likely to buy your product or service.

3. Determine what value(s) would appeal to that audience. How are you going to incorporate that value into your ad?

4. Make up a slogan, using one of the idioms from this chapter.

5. Decide what visual cues (pictures, etc.) will accompany the slogan.

6. Write the rest of the ad.

7. Present it to the class. Do you think this ad would appeal to the other members of your class?

PROBLEM SOLVING

Idioms
OPEN A CAN OF WORMS
BLOW IT
IN OVER ONE'S HEAD
KEEP A LEVEL HEAD
CUT CORNERS
SLIP ONE'S MIND
TILL THE COWS COME HOME
THROW IN THE TOWEL
RIGHT AROUND THE CORNER
CROSS THAT BRIDGE WHEN ONE COMES TO IT
GET SOMETHING OFF THE GROUND
OFF THE TOP OF ONE'S HEAD
ODDS ARE

I Learning the Idioms

WARMING UP

Do the following activities in small groups of three to five students.
Compare answers and discuss with your classmates.

1. With the other members of your group, make a list of the five best inventions or developments of the twentieth century. Put a check next to the one you think was the most significant.

2. Imagine you are living in the year 2100. How is life different from now? Discuss the ways you think life will change in the next century. Talk about school, home life, entertainment, transportation, fashion, medicine, work, and so on. Write down what you think the ten most significant changes will be. Indicate whether you think each is a change for the better or for the worse.

3. Read the following statements about life in the year 2100. Decide if you agree or disagree. Then ask three of your classmates if they agree or disagree.

    AGREE   DISAGREE

    a. _____ _____ People will have to wear special clothing and oxygen masks to protect them from the poisonous environment.

    b. _____ _____ Doctors will have found a cure for most diseases, including cancer and AIDS.

    c. _____ _____ There will be a single world government.

    d. _____ _____ Parents will be able to choose the sex of their children.

    e. _____ _____ English will be the official world language.

    f. _____ _____ Much of the world will have been destroyed by the Third and Fourth World Wars.

    g. _____ _____ The United States will no longer be one of the world's superpowers.

    h. _____ _____ People will live in space stations or on other planets.

    i. _____ _____ Robots will be as common as telephones are today.

    j. _____ _____ People will be able to travel through time.

4. If you could visit any period of time for one day, would you travel to the past or to the future? Why? Take a quick survey among your classmates to find out if they would prefer going forward or backward in time. Is the past or the future more popular? Why? How far back or forward would you like to go?

GETTING TO KNOW THE IDIOMS

A. Listening for Understanding

Listen to the following conversation between two characters in a movie about time travel. Consider these questions as you listen to their conversation. Afterward, discuss the answers with your classmates in pairs or small groups.

1. What is Alfred trying to do? Why is it so difficult?

2. Why is Bernie so nervous and anxious for Alfred to succeed?

3. Who do you think Betsy is?

4. What do you think happened before this scene?

5. What do you think happened after Bernie put the wires together?

6. How do you think this movie will end?

B. Identifying the Idioms

Next, read the script to which you have just listened. Throughout the conversation you will find the idioms listed below. Underline the idioms, and number them on the list in the order in which you find them. Can you tell what they mean by how they are used?

_____ **keep a level head**

_____ **right around the corner**

_____ **slip one's mind**

_____ **get something off the ground**

_____ **off the top of one's head**

_____ **cut corners**

_____ **cross that bridge when one comes to it**

_____ **open a can of worms**

_____ **throw in the towel**

_____ **till the cows come home**

_____ **blow it**

_____ **in over one's head**

_____ **odds are**

IN OVER THEIR HEADS

A scene from the movie Time After Time, *a science-fiction drama about travelers through time.*

BERNIE: Did you call Dr. Bleeb?

ALFRED: No, it slipped my mind.

BERNIE: It slipped your mind? Alfred, this is urgent! I've only got two more days to get back to Russia in 1867. If I don't make it, I may never see Betsy again. This is my last chance. Please don't blow it for me!

ALFRED: Bernie, I don't know if I can help you. I'm doing my best, but I think I'm in over my head this time. Time travel is too complicated, too unpredictable. If hundreds of brilliant scientists haven't been able to do it before now, I probably won't either. I'm just not sure it's possible.

BERNIE: But you said that success was right around the corner. You said that any day there would be a breakthrough. We've got the technology; someone just has to get lucky. Alfred, think of what this could do for you professionally! They'd probably hand you the Nobel Prize. And besides, Betsy's life depends on it! You *have* to get this project off the ground!

ALFRED: Look, Bernie, you've got to calm down. Odds are, there is no way to get there from here. But you've got to believe I'm trying. I can't cut corners; there are certain steps that I have to follow every time I try to reconfigure the neutrons, and it takes time.

BERNIE: I'm sorry, Alfred, you're right. I've got to keep a level head. I know it's not easy, but I believe if anybody can do it, you can.

ALFRED: The problem is that there is no way to predict what is going to happen each time I try something new. I could work on this till the cows come home and not come any closer than I am now to real time travel. And whenever I experiment with a different equation, there's a whole new set of problems. It's like opening a can of worms. Who knows—I might accidentally blow up the world.

BERNIE: Please don't throw in the towel. You can't give up! Think about Betsy. She's lost in another century. Think how lonely she must feel. What if we don't find her? What if we can't get there in time?

ALFRED: Don't worry about that now. We'll cross that bridge when we come to it.

BERNIE: Hey, Alfred, off the top of your head, do you know what would happen if I put these two wires together? I can't tell what they're attached to.

ALFRED: **NO! DON'T TOUCH THOSE WI. . . .**

C. Getting the Meaning

Notice the highlighted phrase in each of the following statements. Pay attention to how the idiom is used, and try to guess its meaning. You may also refer to the preceding conversation. Write the meaning of the idiom on the line. The first one is done for you.

1. I was going to get the car keys from my husband, but it **slipped my mind**.

   to forget something you were supposed to remember

2. The crash at the air show was apparently the result of pilot error. He should have pulled out of his dive earlier, but he **blew it.**

3. I don't understand a thing in my chemistry class. I'm definitely **in over my head**.

4. We have the technology now to create an artificial environment, so space cities seem to be **right around the corner.**

5. There's a lot of opposition to the school's bilingual program. We'll need more parental support to **get it off the ground**.

6. Don't worry about the stain on the tablecloth. **Odds are** no one will even notice it.

7. After one floor of the Lakeview Hotel collapsed, the owners realized that the construction company had tried to save time and money by **cutting corners**.

8. If the lawyers start attacking your testimony, remember to **keep a level head**. Try to think, and answer their questions clearly and calmly.

9. I'm sure Joe is not coming today. I could wait **till the cows come home**, and he still wouldn't be here.

10. Some people say that letting women fully participate in the military would be **opening a can of worms**.

   _____

11. I give up! I'm never going to get this engine to work, so I'm **throwing in the towel**.

   _____

12. It's silly to worry about what you're going to wear to the dance before you've even been invited to go. You can **cross that bridge when you come to it**.

   _____

13. **Off the top of your head**, can you remember the name of that movie we saw starring Robert Redford and Paul Newman?

   _____

PRACTICING THE IDIOMS

D. Choosing the Best Answer

Listen carefully to the following taped statements. Read the choices listed below for each statement you hear. Select the sentence that best relates to the original statement, and circle the corresponding letter.

1. a. I will be upset if you forget our anniversary.
   b. You have always remembered our anniversary in the past.

2. a. Even if Jenny makes a mistake, she'll win the medal.
   b. Jenny must perform a very good dive.

3. a. In order to fix the engine, he must put his head under the hood of the car.
   b. Calvin doesn't know much about engines.

4. a. The Wright brothers designed their first successful flying machine very soon thereafter.
   b. The Wright brothers invented the airplane a long time after that.

5. a. We're going to have to move it to a different location.
   b. We need a lot of help from members of the community.

6. a. A majority of people will probably vote for the president.
   b. It seems evident that the public is dissatisfied with the current administration.

7. a. You must allow time for the dough to rise.
    b. The corners on each loaf of bread should be even and smooth.

8. a. If Gina had not been thinking clearly, we might still be lost!
    b. We were all calm and unworried except Gina.

9. a. I would probably do poorly on the test anyway.
    b. It's best to study late at night.

10. a. Cindy is hesitant to talk about her divorce.
    b. Her reaction is likely to be very negative; you'll wish you hadn't asked.

11. a. Louis quit trying to get a date.
    b. The women ignored Louis's request for a clean towel.

12. a. You can travel after your grandfather is gone.
    b. You shouldn't be concerned about his death before it actually happens.

13. a. Sabrina easily forgets numbers.
    b. Sabrina doesn't need a calculator to help her add.

E. Retelling the Story—Optional Activity

Read the movie script on pages 40–41 again. The sentences below refer to statements in that script. On the lines below, restate the sentences, using the appropriate idiom. The first one is done for you.

1. When Bernie asks Alfred if he called Dr. Bleeb, Alfred says that he forgot.

    When Bernie asks Alfred if he called Dr. Bleeb, Alfred replies that it

    slipped his mind.

2. Bernie is very concerned that Alfred will ruin his chances of seeing Betsy again.

3. Alfred thinks he is involved in something that is beyond his ability to control.

4. Bernie is under the impression that success is imminent.

5. In order to save Betsy, they have to launch their time travel experiment successfully.

6. There is a good chance that time travel is impossible.

   _____

7. In order to conduct his experiments properly, Alfred simply cannot compromise his standards; he has to complete every step thoroughly and correctly.

   _____

8. Bernie needs to calm down and think rationally.

   _____

9. It is possible that Alfred might work on his project for a very, very long time without finding a solution.

   _____

10. Every time Alfred tries a different approach, he has to contend with another, different, set of problems.

    _____

11. Bernie does not want Alfred to quit.

    _____

12. If they don't succeed, Alfred and Bernie will figure out what to do about Betsy when the time comes.

    _____

13. Bernie asks Alfred if he happens to know what would occur if he put two wires together.

    _____

F. Putting the Idioms into Practice

You are part of a volunteer rescue team that has been sent out to look for a group of lost hikers up in the mountains. The hikers left yesterday morning and were expected back within five or six hours, but they never returned to their camp. Now their families and friends are very worried that something terrible might have happened to them. You must find them before it's too late! The leader of your rescue party has given you some instructions. Substitute one of the idioms listed below for each of the numbered phrases. Remember to change the idioms as needed to fit the sentences.

cut corners	in over one's head
blow it	right around the corner
off the top of one's head	cross that bridge when one comes to it
open a can of worms	odds are
till the cows come home	get something off the ground
throw in the towel	slip one's mind
keep a level head	

First of all, I'd like to thank you for coming. Without your help, this rescue operation could never _____ . I hope this won't take long; if we all do what we're supposed
<u>1. get started</u>

to, the hikers' rescue should be _____ . Remember that you're searching for very
<u>2. here soon</u>

inexperienced hikers, so they are probably _____ . They really
<u>3. unable to deal with the situation</u>

_____ when they left the marked trail, and by now they have realized that
<u>4. made a big mistake</u>

by wandering off without a map or guide, they have _____ .
<u>5. lost control of the situation</u>

_____ that they are scared. _____ to take enough food and
<u>6. Chances are pretty good</u>   <u>7. They probably forgot</u>

supplies for more than a few hours, so you should also expect them to be cold and

hungry. Obviously, the most important thing to do while you're looking for them is to

_____ . Make sure that you search the area carefully and methodi-
<u>8. remain calm and think clearly</u>

cally. You must not _____ ; their lives depend on you. Everyone is
<u>9. do an incomplete job</u>

equipped with two-way radios, so you can let the others know if you find anything.

And if you happen to think of something _____ that you believe might help,
<u>10. spontaneously</u>

tell the other volunteers as soon as possible. We will continue to search _____ ,
<u>11. until very late</u>

so please don't _____ until everyone has been found. If we don't find them tonight
<u>12. quit</u>

. . . well, we'll _____ . Good luck!
<u>13. decide what to do when that time comes</u>

II Finding the Idioms in Ads

INTERPRETING THE ADS

Look at the following advertisements. First determine what is being advertised and what idiom is featured in the ad. Review the meaning of the idiom. Then answer the questions corresponding to each ad.

1. Describe the picture. How does it relate to the idiom?

2. How is a bad haircut "a real can of worms"?

1. In what way is the man in the picture "in over his head"?

2. Is the meaning of "get in over your head" literal or idiomatic? Explain.

3. Near the end of the text it says, "This time, you're in deep." Can you explain the meaning of the idiom "in deep"?

1. What is a *farmhand*? To whom does "farmhands" refer in this ad?

2. Why did the advertisers use farm imagery and language in this ad?

3. Can you rephrase the question, "Where can little farmhands build till the cows come home" using nonidiomatic language?

Fifteen dealerships into their search for a new car, BARRY AND CYNTHIA NELSON felt like throwing in the towel.

Then Cynthia's mother suggested us. She'd heard we were a brand new company, and that our cars cost about the same as all the imports they'd been looking at.

So Barry and Cynthia dropped into a Saturn showroom, prepared to do battle with the sales staff and ready to just wash their hands of the whole idea of buying a new car. But the showroom staff took the Nelsons completely by surprise, as they have just about all of our customers.

How? Well, it's pretty simple—from one end of Saturn to the other, it all comes down to this: we're different. (In fact, there's a ton of research about how we're changing the automobile business. Especially the way we take care of our customers. But since other car companies are always quoting this report or that one, we'll just quote Barry.)

"I've never been a joiner, I'm not in any clubs or anything. But this—you know, I wave at every Saturn that goes by, and they wave right back. It feels like we're related or something. And the weird thing is—all I did was buy a car."

A DIFFERENT KIND *of* COMPANY. A DIFFERENT KIND *of* CAR.
If you'd like to know more about Saturn, and our new sedans and coupe, please call us at 1-800-522-5000.

M.S.R.P. for base Saturn cars range from $8,795 to $11,875 including retailer preparation. Tax, license, options and transportation charges additional. The Nelsons are pictured with a 1992 Saturn SL2. ©1992 Saturn Corporation.

1. Why did the Nelsons feel like "throwing in the towel"?

2. Did they quit looking for a car? What happened?

1. What does it mean to "count calories"? What are "reps"? What does it mean to "count reps"? What kind of person would count calories and reps?

2. Can you explain the meaning of "You'd rather lose than be a spectator"?

3. How could someone in the situation described in the ad "blow it"?

THINKING ABOUT THE ADS

Review the ads from this chapter. Based on the messages contained in the ads, choose the one that you think best illustrates American cultural values. Complete statements one through four based on that ad.

1. This ad would appeal to an American audience because . . . .

2. It is important to many Americans to . . . .

3. Other examples in American life that show how Americans feel about this issue or value are . . . .

4. This ad would/would not appeal to an audience from my country because . . . .

5. The ad that I liked the best is . . . .

6. The ad that made the best use of an idiom is . . . because . . . .

III Using the Idioms

USING THE IDIOMS IN SPEECH

A. One-minute Speech

Write a brief outline before presenting your one-minute speech to your classmates. Be sure to use the idioms from this chapter in your speech.

Think of a time in your life when you had to go through a difficult, frightening, or painful experience (for example, sustaining a physical injury, being in a car accident, being threatened by someone, facing an unusual challenge at work or school). Can you describe the situation? What did you do? Do you think you handled the problem well? How was the situation resolved? Explain your experience to the other members of your group.

B. Group Discussion

Participate in the following discussion, using the idioms from this chapter.

Shipwrecked! Your wonderful vacation on a luxurious cruise ship came to an abrupt end when the ship ran into a submerged rock and started to sink. You and the other members of your group were able to jump into a lifeboat, but it's not very sturdy, and you don't know how long you can last out in the middle of the ocean. You and your fellow travelers are split into two groups: those who are optimistic about your chances of survival, and those who are pessimistic and don't think you can make it. Decide who will be on either side, and discuss the following questions:

- When do you think you will be rescued?

- How will you stay alive until help comes?

- How will you ration the small amount of water and food in the lifeboat?

- What are your chances of survival?

- What will you do if you are not found soon?

C. Debate: Genetic engineering

Read the situation and choose to defend either side of the following question: Should genetic engineering be allowed? *Before you begin, jot down the arguments supporting your position. Remember to use as many of the idioms from this chapter as you can.*

Through recent advances in a technical field called genetic engineering, scientists have been able to manipulate the DNA, or genetic material of life, so that they can in effect create new life forms in a laboratory. This ability to change genetic molecules for various purposes has been the subject of much controversy. Proponents of genetic engineering say that it offers the hope of a permanent cure for many inherited illnesses. It makes possible the growth of "perfect" fruits, vegetables, and other foods that are resistant to disease or decay. Genetically altered bacteria provide a common treatment for cancer. These are only a few examples of what is and might be possible in this new and exciting field. Scientists are only beginning to realize the tremendous potential of this technology.

However, not everyone agrees that this field should be explored any further. While the benefits may be considerable, genetic engineering is also potentially very dangerous. If genes can be altered in "good" ways, so can they be changed to create new diseases and new environmental hazards. Opponents say that genetic engineering is "playing God" and that all life forms, even imperfect ones, should be left alone. They say that humans cannot possibly accurately estimate the results or consequences of experimentation with the genes of living organisms, and that it is only a matter of time before something disastrous happens.

D. Role Plays

Imagine yourself in one of the situations described below. Act it out with another member of your class, using as many idioms from this chapter as you can in your conversation. You and your partner may want to write a brief script of the role play before acting it out.

1. (two friends)

FRIEND A: You *love to* play the lottery! Although you have never actually won anything, you are sure you will hit the jackpot very soon. It's true that you do spend a whole lot of money on your hobby, but you firmly believe that if you play long enough, you will get rich.

FRIEND B: Your friend can't understand how much control this urge to gamble has on his/her life. Try to convince your friend to think rationally about what he/she is doing; the chances of winning any money at all are very slight. If your friend wants to get rich, there's no way to take shortcuts; one must just work hard like the rest of society, and not waste any more money on the lottery! Your friend might play every day for a lifetime and not make a dime! Tell your friend to quit now, before it's too late.

2. (Alfred, Bernie)

ALFRED: You *told* Bernie not to touch those wires! Now he has really made a mess of things! He made a big mistake, and you don't think your chances of fixing it are very good. What are you going to do? Talk to Bernie about your situation.

BERNIE: You *must* remain calm. There must be some way out of this mess, but you can't think of what it might be. If you and Alfred work together, you can probably get things back to the way they were. Discuss your situation with Alfred.

USING THE IDIOMS IN WRITING

E. Writing with Idioms

Write a letter in response to the situation described below, using as many idioms from this chapter as possible.

You are the agent for a very talented and promising musician. It seems evident to you that very soon your client will be a huge star, but it is very difficult to get started in the music industry, and so far the musician has had no luck. You were aware that your client was feeling quite discouraged, but still you were quite surprised to receive the following letter from him/her.

> May 19, 1994
>
> Mr. David Bashaw
> Beautiful Noise Industries
> 485 Wilcox Street
> Los Angeles, CA 90087
>
> Dear Mr. Bashaw:
>   I appreciate very much the work you've done on my behalf during the past four years. You have contacted most of the major recording studios, introduced me to some very influential people in the business, sent out dozens of demo tapes that I recorded, and widely publicized my music in other ways as well. I don't doubt that you have done your job quite thoroughly. However, after all this time, I still have not been able to get a recording contract. I will have a hard time paying my bills if I continue to try to make a living as a musician. Because I feel that it's time to move on with my life, I hereby notify you that I must terminate my association with your agency. Thank you for all of your help. I wish you better luck with your other clients.
>
>   Sincerely,
>
>   Chris Jenkins

How will you respond? Should you encourage your client to keep on trying, or do you agree that it is time to give up?

F. Advertising with Idioms

Make up an advertisement for any type of product not *advertised in the ads in this chapter, using one (or more) of the idioms you have just learned. Follow the steps listed below.*

1. Choose a product or service that you would like to advertise.

2. Determine your *audience*—the people most likely to buy your product or service.

3. Determine what value(s) would appeal to that audience. How are you going to incorporate that value into your ad?

4. Make up a slogan, using one of the idioms from this chapter.

5. Decide what visual cues (pictures, etc.) will accompany the slogan.

6. Write the rest of the ad.

7. Present it to the class. Do you think this ad would appeal to the other members of your class?

MAKING AN IMPRESSION

Idioms

- MAKE A MARK
- TAKE CENTER STAGE
- HANDS DOWN
- HAVE A CORNER ON SOMETHING
- STRIKE A CHORD
- **FEATHER IN ONE'S CAP**
- AHEAD OF ONE'S TIME
- BRING TO ONE'S FEET
- PUT ONE'S NAME ON THE LINE
- RAISE EYEBROWS
- OFF THE BEATEN PATH
- WARM UP TO
- HAND OVER FIST
- FLASH IN THE PAN

I Learning the Idioms

WARMING UP

1. Select three famous people from any time period. Write their names in the chart below, at the top of each of the three columns. Then walk around the classroom, asking several of your classmates to tell you *one* thing they know about each of the people on your list. Their comments should be brief enough to write on one line. After you have compiled a list of biographical data on your group of famous people, present the information to the class.

	Famous Person	**Famous Person**	**Famous Person**
Time Period			
Country:			
Profession:			
Claim to Fame:			
Other			

2. Think of a famous character in history. Tell the class the initials (the first letter of the first and last name) of this character, and write those initials on the chalkboard. Your classmates will then ask you questions requiring either *yes* or *no* as an answer to try to determine who it is. For example, "Is this person alive today?" "Is this a real person?" "Is this person a woman?" Whoever correctly guesses the name of the character will provide the next set of initials for the class.

3. In a small group of three to five students, make a list of ten famous people, past or present. If you had a chance to talk to these people, what questions would you ask them? Next to each name, write down one question you would ask if you could speak with that person. Share your list and questions with the rest of the class.

GETTING TO KNOW THE IDIOMS

A. Listening for Understanding

Listen to the following descriptions of two famous characters, and try to guess their identities. Consider these questions as you listen to the descriptions. Afterward, discuss the answers with your classmates in pairs or small groups.

1. How did Mystery Character 1 achieve fame in the film industry?

2. Why do you think some people were skeptical of his ideas?

3. What were the two major attractions that he conceived and built?

4. How long has Mystery Character 2 been around?

5. Is he still popular? With whom especially?

6. If you were going to make a cartoon character of an animal, what type of animal would you choose?

B. Identifying the Idioms

Next, read the descriptions to which you have just listened. Throughout these descriptions you will find the idioms listed below. Underline the idioms, and number them on the list in the order in which you find them. Can you tell what they mean by how they are used?

_____ have a corner on something	_____ feather in one's cap
_____ raise eyebrows	_____ ahead of one's time
_____ hands down	_____ make a mark
_____ hand over fist	_____ off the beaten path
_____ take center stage	_____ put one's name on the line
_____ strike a chord	_____ bring to one's feet
_____ flash in the pan	_____ warm up to

GUESS WHO?

Mystery Character 1

This is a man who was recognized for his creative genius, and who revolutionized the film and entertainment industry. He was ahead of his time, when, in the early 1920s, he established his own company to produce the animated motion pictures for which he became famous. Soon after, he was making money hand over fist from the increasingly popular cartoon characters he had created, and he quickly had a corner on the market of animated films. Not satisfied with his early accomplishments, however, he began to envision an empire that would completely transform the world of entertainment. After borrowing millions of dollars, he put his name on the line to bring his dreams to life, and ultimately he succeeded in building the largest and most famous amusement park on earth. He created a world within a world, a place where adults could become children once again, and explore the adventures awaiting in Fantasyland, or Tomorrowland, or Frontierland. Although there were many who originally thought he was too far off the beaten path to appeal to a broad audience, he effectively silenced his critics with the tremendous success of his theme park. Later, he built a similar attraction in Florida, which proved to be another feather in his cap. During his lifetime, he also won thirty-nine Academy Awards for his work in the film industry. He died in 1966, but he continues to make a mark on the world of entertainment. The empire he built keeps growing and inspiring other dreamers to believe that with a little imagination, anything is possible!

Mystery Character 2

This is perhaps the most famous movie star of all time. He appeared in his first motion picture, *Steamboat Willie*, in 1928, and he is even more popular today than he was back then. Although he probably raised a few eyebrows when he was first introduced to audiences around the world, the public soon warmed up to him. His character especially struck a chord with children, and he was immediately embraced and loved by children everywhere. It was not long before he could win any popularity contest hands down; there was even a television show created for his fan clubs. Today his fame continues to spread. In fact, little statues of this extraordinary star are nearly as numerous as crucifixes and statues of Buddha, and over five thousand products in the world have his image on them. After more than a half-century of celebrity status, he has proved that he was not just a flash in the pan. Everywhere he appears, he takes center stage; no matter where in the world he goes, he brings people of all ages to their feet. Best of all, he is not selfish or egotistical like many of today's celebrities—he gives full credit for his success to the man who created him, and he generously shares his fame with his wife, Minnie, and his good friends Goofy and Pluto.

C. Getting the Meaning

Notice the highlighted phrase in each of the following sentences. Pay attention to how the idiom is used, and try to guess its meaning. You may also refer to the preceding descriptions. Write the meaning of the idiom on the line. The first one is done for you.

1. The prima ballerina Marie Taglioni was **ahead of her time** when she devised a way to dance on her toes. From that time on, ballet took on a delicate and ethereal new form.

   new and revolutionary in concept

2. Fifteen years ago, I never imagined I would be making money **hand over fist** from my stock in Micromagic.

3. There is no other architectural design company in this area. We've got **a corner on the market**.

_____

4. Mr. Krebs believed in the innocence of his client; otherwise he never would have **put his name on the line** to defend a convicted murderer.

_____

5. You would be foolish to listen to Jared. His ideas are always too far **off the beaten path** to be taken seriously.

_____

6. Congratulations on your big promotion! That's a real **feather in your cap**!

_____

7. Jackie Robinson **made a mark** on professional baseball when he became the first African American admitted to play in the major leagues.

_____

8. Susie's dress was rather tight fitting and low cut. I'm sure she **raised some eyebrows** at the council meeting.

_____

9. I know that Boston wasn't your first choice for finding a job, but I think that in time you'll **warm up to** the city.

_____

10. I was deeply moved by the preacher's sermon. Something about his message really **struck a chord**.

_____

11. Playing one-on-one, I think Michael Jordan could beat any other basketball player **hands down**.

_____

12. Everyone predicted that rock-and-roll music would be a **flash in the pan**, but it has remained popular for nearly half a century.

_____

13. I hate going out in public with my sister. With her flashy clothes and outgoing personality she **takes center stage** wherever she goes.

_____

14. The soprano in the opera was superb. She **brought the crowd to its feet** several times during the second act.

_____

PRACTICING THE IDIOMS

D. Choosing the Best Answer

Listen carefully to the following taped statements. Read the choices listed below for each statement you hear. Select the sentence that best relates to the original statement, and circle the corresponding letter.

1. a. Before he started manufacturing automobiles, horse-drawn carriages were thought to be the best mode of transportation.
   b. At that time the concept of traveling in automobiles was common and widespread.

2. a. The new business James started is quite profitable.
   b. The new business James started is failing.

3. a. The Democrats lose most elections in Utah.
   b. Few of the elected officials in Utah are Republicans.

4. a. The mob might have killed Anna.
   b. Anna wanted to change her life, so she decided to join the protesters.

5. a. The settlers could easily get the supplies they needed.
   b. The settlement was not close to any other civilized area.

6. a. Because she had won other awards, the Oscar nomination probably didn't mean much to her.
   b. The Oscar is a very prestigious award.

7. a. The Fishers were quiet and mostly kept to themselves.
   b. This community is different from the way it was before they came.

8. a. It was not surprising that some members of Congress were shocked at his plan.
   b. Everyone was in favor of the proposal.

9. a. You will probably really enjoy scuba diving after a while.
    b. The water in the Caribbean is warmer than in other places.

10. a. Because she deals with art all day, she is probably tired of talking about it.
    b. She was very interested in what you were saying.

11. a. There is no doubt that Teresa would win.
    b. Teresa cheats when she plays chess.

12. a. The popularity of many styles from the sixties lasted a long time.
    b. Fashion trends usually come and go very quickly.

13. a. Eddie usually gets a lot of attention.
    b. Most people don't pay any attention to six-year-old children.

14. a. The people were very angry at what he was saying.
    b. The message that he delivered was very well received.

E. Retelling the Story— Optional Activity

Read the descriptions on pages 58–59 again. The sentences below refer to statements in those descriptions. On the lines below, restate the sentences, using the appropriate idiom. The first one is done for you.

1. Walt Disney was revolutionary in his approach to movie making.

   Walt Disney was ahead of his time in the movie industry.
   _____

2. Shortly after establishing his own production company, he was making a lot of money very quickly on his animated motion pictures.

   _____

3. Soon he had a monopoly on the production of animated films.

   _____

4. Disney borrowed a lot of money and risked his reputation to build Disneyland.

   _____

5. Many people thought he was not in touch with the interests of the majority when he built Disneyland, but the success of the venture proved them wrong.

   _____

6. The completion of Disney world in Florida proved to be an added accomplishment of which he was very proud.

   _____

7. Even after his death, Walt Disney continues to have an impact on the world of entertainment.

   _____

8. The character of Mickey Mouse probably caused some surprise and disapproval at first.

   _____

9. Soon, however, audiences began to like him more and more.

   _____

10. He especially appealed to children.

    _____

11. He could beat any other celebrity in a popularity contest easily.

    _____

12. His continuing fame has proved that Mickey Mouse is not a passing fad.

    _____

13. Everywhere he appears, Mickey Mouse gets a lot of attention from the people around him.

    _____

14. He is such a popular character that audiences often stand and cheer for him.

    _____

F. Putting the Idioms into Practice

Read the following descriptions of famous people. First determine which of the following idioms correctly fits in the blank in each paragraph. Then, choosing from the list of characters below, try to guess who the person is.

LIST OF IDIOMS

hands down
ahead of his time
took center stage
strike a chord
feather in her cap
made a mark
flash in the pan
hand over fist
raised some eyebrows
put his reputation on the line
have a corner on
warmed up to
bring audiences to their feet
off the beaten path

LIST OF CHARACTERS

Rudolph Valentino
Cleopatra VII
Marco Polo
Vincent van Gogh
Lieutenant Hiroo Onoda
Elizabeth Taylor
Michael Jackson
Charles A. Lindbergh Jr.
Elvis Presley
Babe Ruth
Henry Ford II
Jim Henson
Alfred Bernhard Nobel
Lady Godiva

1. This Anglo-Saxon noblewoman ———————— when she persuaded her husband to lower the taxes on the people of Coventry by agreeing to ride naked on a white horse through the town.

   Who is this person? ————————

2. In 1983 one very famous and popular performer seemed to ———————— nominations for the Grammy Award, given to the best musicians of the year in different categories. Nominated for a record-breaking twelve Grammies, he won eight—more than anyone had ever won in a single year.

   Who is this person? ————————

3. In 1926, a handsome Italian-born American film actor died unexpectedly at the age of thirty-one. In spite of his youth, he had obviously ———————— on the world of cinema. Over one hundred thousand fans attended his funeral, while millions more, mostly women, grieved for the loss of a romantic idol.

   Who is this person? ————————.

4. The man who won the title of "The Greatest Baseball Player in History" _____ had a habit of wearing a cabbage leaf beneath his baseball cap to keep his head cool on hot days.

   Who is this person? _____

5. The inventor of dynamite earned his fortune _____ by manufacturing explosives. However, he is better known for providing in his will for the major portion of his 9 million-dollar estate to be set up as a fund to establish yearly prizes for outstanding work in such areas as physics, medicine, literature, and world peace.

   Who is this person? _____

6. One of the most amazing stories to come out of World War II concerns this Japanese soldier who hid in the Philippine jungles and stayed _____ for twenty-nine years to avoid being caught. He did not know the war was over!

   Who is this person? _____

7. The puppets created by this man _____ with millions of people young and old. Including such beloved characters as Kermit the Frog, Miss Piggy, and Bert and Ernie, his Muppets are world famous.

   Who is this person? _____

8. After the Second World War the British offered the German Volkswagen plant to this famous car maker for free. However, because he was concerned about how the acquisition would be perceived by his fellow Americans, this man was unwilling to _____ , and he refused to take it.

   Who is this person? _____

9. This famous American rock-and-roll singer, known as "The King," never failed to _____ throughout his career. Few people know that he was a twin. His brother, Jessie Garon, died at birth in 1935.

   Who is this person? _____

10. This man was certainly _____ when he introduced Europeans to ice cream made with milk. He had obtained the idea from the Chinese court of Kublai Khan.

    Who is this person? _____

11. Many Hollywood marriages are a _____ and are seldom expected to last long. One of the best examples of this phenomenon is that of this famous actress who has been married eight times. Two of those marriages were to the same man, Richard Burton.

    Who is this person? _____

12. In 1932 the kidnapping and murder of this nineteen-month-old child _____ in the media; news reports called it "The Crime of the Century." The child's father, a famous aviator and Pulitzer Prize winner, and his mother, a well-known writer, moved to Europe to avoid further publicity after the murderer was found guilty and executed.

    Who is this person? _____

13. Although his postimpressionistic artwork was not very popular while he was living, since his death in 1890 the public has _____ this artist's innovative style and use of color. In 1990 his *Portrait of Dr. Gachet* was auctioned off for a record $82.5 million to a Japanese businessman.

    Who is this person? _____

14. She was exiled by her brother when she was twenty years old, but this woman's later triumphal return to power as the final ruler of the Ptolemies' dynasty in Egypt was a real _____ . She is also famous for deciding to kill herself by snakebite after hearing reports that her husband, Mark Antony, had been defeated in battle and had committed suicide.

    Who is this person? _____

II Finding the Idioms in Ads

INTERPRETING THE ADS

Look at the following advertisements. First determine what is being advertised and what idiom is featured in the ad. Review the meaning of the idiom. Then answer the questions corresponding to each ad.

1. How is this toothbrush "ahead of its time"?

2. What is this man's problem? How can this toothbrush help him?

3. What does "just in time" mean? Why is the toothbrush just in time for this man?

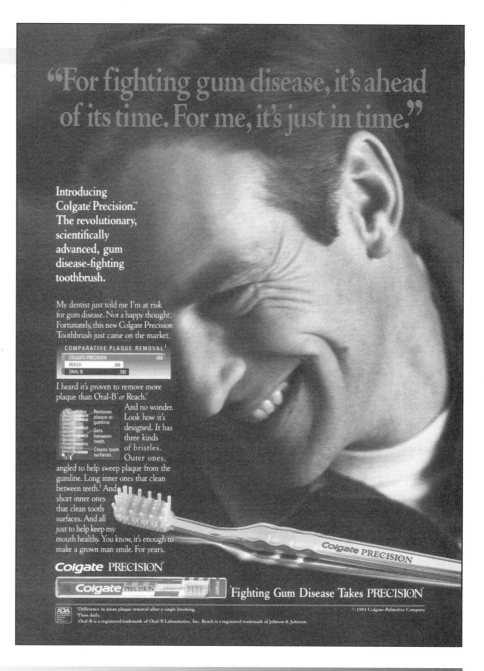

1. Describe the picture. What does it have to do with the line "We've got a corner on great tasting side dishes"?

2. Is that line used idiomatically or literally?

1. What type of hat is pictured in this ad? Can you describe it? With what country would you associate this type of hat?

2. Why is a European route a feather in the airline's cap?

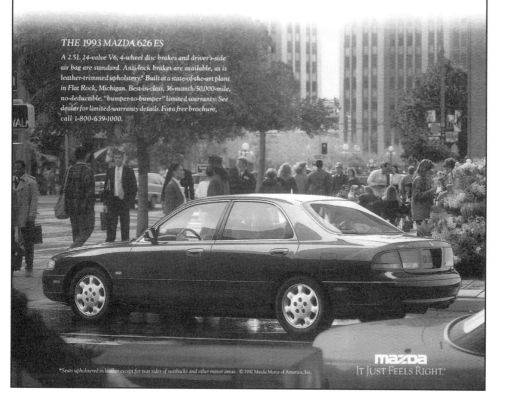

GET OFF THE BEATEN PATH WITHOUT LEAVING TOWN. If you love driving, you're always looking for a better way to get from here to there. That's the philosophy behind the 1993 Mazda 626 ES. Because in a class of cars that strives to be average, this car has unique virtues and a character all its own. ❀ Its elegant exterior echoes the curves of a coastal highway, while the interior cradles you in comfort and security. A 24-valve, aluminum alloy V6 is one of the smoothest, quietest piston engines in the world. And an agile suspension gives you the advantage in tight traffic. Harmony of style and performance set this new 626 apart. Qualities that are at the heart of every Mazda. ❀ So take to the road in the all-new Mazda 626 ES. And discover how it feels to go your own way every time you turn the key.

THE 1993 MAZDA 626 ES

A 2.5L 24-valve V6, 4-wheel disc brakes and driver's-side air bag are standard. Anti-lock brakes are available, as is leather-trimmed upholstery.* Built at a state-of-the-art plant in Flat Rock, Michigan. Best-in-class, 36-month/50,000-mile, no-deductible, "bumper-to-bumper" limited warranty. See dealer for limited-warranty details. For a free brochure, call 1-800-639-1000.

*Seats upholstered in leather except for rear sides of seatbacks and other minor areas. © 1992 Mazda Motor of America, Inc.

mazda
IT JUST FEELS RIGHT.®

1. Does "off the beaten path" in this ad refer to a place? What does it refer to?

2. The last line of text summarizes the message of this ad: "And discover how it feels to go your own way every time you turn the key." Can you explain what that means?

1. The graph in the ad shows the average annual return on financial investments. How does Alltel compare with other companies?

2. The other companies' returns are depicted with an ordinary bar graph. What do they use to show Alltel's returns? How does that fit in with the line, "We've made quite a mark in our industry"?

1. What are "Heavyhands"?

2. Who is the intended audience for this ad? Is it fitness equipment dealers or consumers?

3. How will buying Heavyhands help them make money?

THINKING ABOUT THE ADS

Review the ads from this chapter. Based on the messages contained in the ads, choose the one that you think best illustrates American cultural values. Complete statements one through four based on that ad.

1. This ad would appeal to an American audience because . . . .

2. It is important to many Americans to . . . .

3. Other examples in American life that show how Americans feel about this issue or value are . . . .

4. This ad would/would not appeal to an audience from my country because . . . .

5. The ad that I liked the best is . . . .

6. The ad that made the best use of an idiom is . . . because . . . .

III Using the Idioms

USING THE IDIOMS IN SPEECH

A. One-minute Speech

Write a brief outline before presenting your one-minute speech to your classmates. Be sure to use the idioms from this chapter in your speech.

Think of a real or fictional character that has had a significant impact on society. You may choose from the list below, or think of one on your own. Why is this character famous? How is he/she remembered today? What do you know about this person's life? Tell about this character and his/her influence on society.

Superman	Karl Marx	Joan of Arc
Sigmund Freud	Pelé	Ludwig van Beethoven
Charles Darwin	Marilyn Monroe	John Wayne
Leonardo da Vinci	Agatha Christie	Snoopy
Mohammed	Marie Curie	Mao Zedong
Christopher Columbus	Socrates	Napoleon Bonaparte

B. Group Discussion

Participate in the following discussion, using the idioms from this chapter.

Edith Cromwell: age 69, Irish immigrant, homemaker, raised six children.

Reginald Thompson: age 26, unmarried, engineer, work associates describe him as "ordinary."

Julia Miller: age 34, nightclub singer, recently spent a few months in jail on a drug charge.

The people described above, Edith Cromwell, Reginald Thompson, and Julia Miller, each did something recently to win fame and widespread publicity. They are all going to appear tonight as guests on a national television talk show. However, the host of the show has lost his notes, and cannot remember what their extraordinary deeds were. You must write a brief summary for each person describing the following points:

- What did this person do?
- What was the public's reaction to this act?
- What effect will it have on society?
- Do you think the media attention will last long?
- What do you think is likely to happen to this person in the future?

C. Debate: Parapsychology

Read the situation and choose to defend either side of the following question: Is investing in a business to sell psychic services a good idea? *Before you begin, jot down the arguments supporting your position. Remember to use as many of the idioms from this chapter as you can.*

The study of parapsychology has always been highly controversial. On one hand, believers cite numerous unexplained phenomena that they claim prove the existence of ghosts and extrasensory powers. On the other hand, nonbelievers point to the lack of hard evidence supporting such claims, noting that it is nearly impossible to duplicate positive results in scientifically controlled experiments.

A close friend of yours who claims to possess psychic powers is interested in establishing a business with your help to promote and sell his services. He thinks that he could be of use in such efforts as locating lost individuals or removing ghosts from a haunted house. Your friend believes that there would be a high demand for his services and that your financial investment in this business would be very safe.

D. Role Plays

Imagine yourself in one of the situations described below. Act it out with another member of your class, using as many idioms from this chapter as you can in your conversation. You and your partner may want to write a brief script of the role play before acting it out.

1. (a biographer who is writing a book on the Beatles, a former manager of the Beatles)

BEATLES BIOGRAPHER: You are writing a book about the Beatles and the phenomenal success of their music, from the time they first appeared on the scene in 1960 until now, decades after the group broke up. During the ten years the group was together, they dominated rock music. Now you have a rare opportunity to interview one of the former managers of the band and ask him about the effect he feels the Beatles had on the young people of his generation.

FORMER BEATLES MANAGER: A lot of people disapproved of the Beatles when they got started, but obviously the world soon accepted and came to love the distinctive sound of the group. You think a lot of fans could relate to the themes of personal and political rebellion the Beatles symbolized. One of your proudest achievements was the album *Sergeant Pepper's Lonely Hearts Club Band* in 1967. You feel certain the Beatles are easily the most popular rock-and-roll band of all time, and their impact on music will last a long time.

2. (Walt Disney, Mickey Mouse)

WALT DISNEY: You are proud of all of your accomplishments, but you believe that your fame has spread most through the giant amusement parks that bear your name. After all, you started with Disneyland in California, and that was followed by Disneyworld, and then Disney parks in Japan and Europe—they're now spreading throughout the world! Although your cartoon characters are important, they have not had the influence that the amusement parks have. Express your point of view.

MICKEY MOUSE: Mr. Disney thinks amusement parks are more important than movies! How could he possibly believe that? It's clear that many more people see movies on a regular basis than go to amusement parks! Movies are obviously more popular! And Disney movies have always had a monopoly on good family entertainment. Mr. Disney never could have succeeded when he built Disneyland had it not been that people were already familiar with his delightful cartoon characters (such as yourself). And those characters have lasted longer and been more famous than any other characters in history. Tell Mr. Disney what you think!

USING THE IDIOMS IN WRITING

E. Writing with Idioms

Write a report based on the situation described below, using the idioms from this chapter.

Imagine it is fifty years from now. A student in a classroom somewhere in the world is about to give a report on a famous person from the past—you! Write the report this student would give. How would you describe the challenges you faced during your lifetime? What successes did you achieve? What did you do better than anyone else? For what will you be remembered? (Remember, your life isn't over—you can be as imaginative as you'd like in describing what you will do in the future.)

F. Advertising with Idioms

Make up an advertisement for any type of product not advertised in the ads in this chapter, using one or more of the idioms you have just learned. Follow the steps listed below.

1. Choose a product or service that you would like to advertise.
2. Determine your audience—the people most likely to buy your product or service.
3. Determine what value(s) would appeal to that audience. How are you going to incorporate that value into your ad?
4. Make up a slogan, using one of the idioms from this chapter.
5. Decide what visual cues (pictures, etc.) will accompany the slogan.
6. Write the rest of the ad.
7. Present it to the class. Do you think this ad would appeal to the other members of your class?

FACING DEFEAT

Lose face.

Save face.

Old Spice

POST SHAVE
CONDITIONER
HYDROGEL

...d you know that every time
...ave, you lose face?
...at's because shaving strips
...in of its protective moisture,
...at can leave it feeling rough, dry
...itated.

That's why you need new Post
Shave Conditioner from Old Spice
after every shave. This remarkable
hydrogel formula saves your face
because it helps restore and maintain
your skin's protective moisture. So
your skin feels smooth and healthy.
And stays that way.

Take the 7-Day Face Test and
prove it to yourself: when it comes to
saving face, new Post Shave Conditioner from Old Spice is the simple
solution.

The simple solution to saving face.

Idioms

UPHILL BATTLE

NOT HAVE A PRAYER

BITE OFF MORE THAN ONE CAN CHEW

SLIP THROUGH ONE'S FINGERS

TOO CLOSE FOR COMFORT

SITTING DUCK

WIPE OUT

STOP SOMETHING IN ITS TRACKS

TAKE IT OUT ON SOMEONE

BRING TO ONE'S KNEES

MISS THE BOAT

SAVE FACE

I Learning the Idioms

WARMING UP

Interview one or two of your classmates from different countries regarding the history and origin of their native land. Use the following questions as a guide.

1. Who were the original settlers of the land that you are from?

2. Was the land they inhabited later invaded by any other group(s) of people? Who?

3. When was the last war fought in your country over territorial rights?

4. Who ultimately won possession of the land?

5. From which group of people did your country get its language and culture?

6. Were there any other races or ethnic groups that significantly influenced your country's customs and culture?

Next, in small groups discuss the following questions.

The United States was founded on the precept that "all men are created equal" (as stated in the Declaration of Independence).

> *We hold these truths to be self-evident: that all men are created equal, that they are endowed by their creator with certain unalienable rights, that among these are life, liberty, and the pursuit of happiness.*

- Do you believe all men (and women) are *treated* equally in the United States? Explain.

- Do you believe all people are treated equally in *your* country? Explain.

- Do you believe a majority of people from your country are prejudiced against any other race or ethnic group? Explain.

- Is discrimination against any other ethnic group or race common in your country? Explain.

GETTING TO KNOW THE IDIOMS

A. Listening for Understanding

Listen to a short history of a bloody period in the American past. Consider these questions as you listen to the historical account. Afterward, discuss the answers with your classmates in pairs or small groups.

1. Who inhabited the American continent when the first European immigrants arrived?

2. How did the settlers feel about these people?

3. The battles on the American frontier during the early 1800s were fought mostly between which two groups?

4. What were they fighting over?

5. What did the American government try to do with the Native Americans?

6. Was this conflict ever resolved? How? Who won?

B. Identifying the Idioms

Next, read the historical account to which you have just listened. Throughout this account you will find the idioms listed below. Underline the idioms, and number them on the list in the order in which you find them. Can you tell what they mean by how they are used?

—— wipe out   —— sitting duck

—— save face   —— too close for comfort

—— uphill battle   —— slip through one's fingers

—— stop something in its tracks   —— not have a prayer

—— miss the boat   —— bite off more than one can chew

—— take it out on someone   —— bring to one's knees

AN UPHILL BATTLE ★ ★ ★ ★ ★

In the early 1800s, Americans began creating the legends of the Wild West by exploring the world that lay beyond their established settlements in the eastern United States. Wagon trains, cowboys herding cattle across wide-open ranges, the Gold Rush, and fiercely independent settlers pushing the frontiers of civilization are all images born of that time of exploration and adventure. The best-known legends of the Wild West, however, sprang from the tales of the cavalry and the Indians, who throughout the nineteenth century were engaged in a war for life and land that ultimately ended in tragedy. In one of the most ill-fated periods of American history, the once proud and powerful Indian nations were almost completely wiped out, betrayed by a government that stole their land in exchange for empty promises.

The early American immigrants were offered cheap and abundant land on the frontier as long as they were willing to settle it. Not wanting to miss the boat, thousands rushed to take advantage of the government's generosity, indifferent to the fact that they were invading Indian territory. Soon, however, they complained that the Indians were too close for comfort. The government tried to remove the tribes by offering them land further west, and while some Indians agreed to move to new land, many resisted the relocation efforts. Those Indians who stayed were sitting ducks; hostility toward them spread quickly throughout the new settlements, and most were killed.

Although a few brave Indian leaders tried desperately to stop the settlers' westward progression in its tracks, fighting back courageously when their territory was invaded, it was an uphill battle, and one that was doomed to failure. Even the few pockets of Indian resistance that somehow slipped through the militia's fingers were at last captured and either killed or forced to move.

More than 70,000 Indians of various tribes finally surrendered to government pressure to leave their homelands and resettle beyond the Mississippi River on the Great Plains, where they were promised sanctuary "as long as trees grow and waters run." The Indians endured so much suffering on that journey that the Cherokee called it the "Trail of Tears."

However, the settlers backed by the U.S Cavalry continued to encroach upon Indian land, and for a brief period, the Indians again fought back. In one famous battle that stood out from the long history of Indian defeat, George Armstrong Custer, with a regiment of 655 men, attacked a Sioux village, resulting in what is commonly called Custer's Last Stand. The officer and his men, tired of the constant skirmishes with their enemies, determined to bring the Indians to their knees. They realized too late, however, that they had bitten off more than they could chew. The village turned out to be a camp of 2,500 to 4,000 Sioux and Cheyenne warriors, who completely overwhelmed and destroyed the regiment. Such battles were rare, though. The white settlers' hatred grew and they continued to take it out on innocent tribal women and children. More and more Indians were killed or sent to live on desolate reservations apart from the settlers. It was not long before the native population, once strong, was decimated.

The final event in the war between the government and the Indians was not a battle; it was a massacre. On December 29, 1890, approximately 300 unarmed Sioux men, women, and children were peacefully gathered at Wounded Knee Creek after their leader, Sitting Bull, was killed. The Indians didn't have a prayer when they were attacked by the heavily armed U.S. Cavalry. While trying to surrender, they were all brutally murdered.

In a final effort to save face, the U.S. government, since 1970, has given back more than 4.5 million acres of Indian land that was wrongfully taken by the white settlers, and it has paid more than $1 billion for land that cannot be returned. The Indians that survive from this bloody period of history are unmoved. Their culture and heritage are nearly extinct. "Now," they say, "there is nothing left. But we must go on. Like the buffalo, we must turn and face the wind." ✯

C. Getting the Meaning

Notice the highlighted phrase in each of the following sentences. Pay attention to how the idiom is used, and try to guess its meaning. You may also refer to the preceding historical account. Write the meaning of the idiom on the line. The first one is done for you.

1. As a result of the vaccine developed by Dr. Jonas Salk, polio was almost completely **wiped out** by the mid-1950s.

   _____eliminate_____

2. If we don't get in line now to buy tickets to the concert, we'll **miss the boat**.

   _____

3. If I had missed one more question on the exam, I wouldn't have passed. That's **too close for comfort**.

   _____

4. Victor was a **sitting duck**. He didn't realize he was playing against a world champion until he had already lost more than $100.

   _____

5. The killer bees are migrating steadily northward toward California, but the Department of Agriculture has guaranteed that it will **stop them in their tracks** before they get there.

   _____

6. Stewart is terrified of the water. Teaching him to swim is an **uphill battle**.

   _____

7. Although the police carefully searched the area, the thieves somehow **slipped through their fingers** once again.

   _____

8. The earthquake destroyed all transportation and communication systems, **bringing the city to its knees**.

   _____

9. Sandy is only a first-year lawyer, but she is representing a multimillion-dollar corporation. I hope she didn't **bite off more than she can chew**.

   _____

10. I know you're angry at your boss, but don't **take it out on me!**

_____

11. The tennis match was between unranked Katy Walker and the reigning champion, Monica Seles. Walker **didn't have a prayer**.

_____

12. Senator Robinson was caught accepting a bribe from a large company. He tried to **save face** by claiming the money was just a loan.

_____

PRACTICING THE IDIOMS

D. Choosing the Best Answer

Listen carefully to the following taped statements. Decide if the sentence that corresponds to each is true or false. Circle T *if it is true and* F *if it is false.*

1. T / F   They need more information about the library fire.

2. T / F   The last contestant probably won the prize.

3. T / F   Some people felt they were in danger from the falling meteor.

4. T / F   Those who were on the front lines could more easily escape harm.

5. T / F   The researchers believe that AIDS will become more prevalent with the passage of time.

6. T / F   The United States will probably soon win many soccer games against the best teams from other countries.

7. T / F   The scientist nearly caught the monster, but it mysteriously escaped.

8. T / F   An alternate source of fuel and energy would be readily available to developed countries.

9. T / F   The entire symphony is too much for Sonya to learn in one month.

10. T / F   It was probably his secretary's fault that Hank lost the account.

11. T / F   The combined United Nations army could most likely win any war.

12. T / F   The wrestler tried to recover his dignity by making excuses for his loss.

E. Retelling the Story—Optional Activity

Read the historical account on pages 78–79 again. The sentences below refer to statements in that account. On the lines below, restate the sentences, using the appropriate idiom. The first one is done for you.

1. During one of the most shameful periods of American history, the American Indians were nearly completely destroyed.

   During a tragic period of history, the American Indians were almost wiped out.

2. The government offered to give the immigrants free land, and many hurried to accept the offer because they didn't want to lose their chance.

3. After moving onto Indian land, the settlers said that the Indians lived dangerously near.

4. The Indians who did not immediately agree to move off their land were in a very vulnerable and unguarded position.

5. A few Indians tried to stop the settlers from moving any further west, but it was a very difficult task.

6. The natives tried to fight back against the settlers, but it was nearly impossible to gain an advantage.

7. The small number of Indians who escaped the army's attempts to force them to move were ultimately caught.

8. Custer wanted to effectively weaken the power of the Indians.

9. The officer and his small army realized that they had tried to do much more than they were capable of when they attacked the Sioux village.

_____

10. The settlers continued to vent their anger and frustration toward the Indians by attacking and killing their women and children.

_____

11. The unarmed Indians at Wounded Knee didn't have any chance of survival against the armed cavalry.

_____

12. Many years later, the American government tried to repair its damaged reputation by giving back Indian land and paying money for land that could not be returned.

_____

F.   Putting the Idioms into Practice

The Health Department is about to issue a warning to the residents of Rocky Bluffs County to notify them that a rare, dangerous, and highly contagious virus has been identified in at least four victims and may be spreading. Health officials are also going to send out the following memo to all doctors and medical personnel in the area. Fill in the blanks with the idioms listed below.

uphill battle	**brought the community to its knees**
too close for comfort	**stop the disease in its tracks**
wipe out	**take it out on**
sitting ducks	**save face**
slip through our fingers	**bitten off more than they can chew**
doesn't have a prayer	**miss the boat**

ALERT!!! This virus could potentially _____ the entire community, so you
                                              1
must diagnose and treat your patients very carefully. Be sure you are aware of all

signs and symptoms the virus may display, or you may _____ and suddenly
                                                            2
find it is too late to help your patients. In that case, your reputation may also be in

danger, and you will not be able to _____ by claiming you were not
                                          3
informed. Remember that early intervention is essential; if the disease goes untreated

for longer than forty-eight hours, the patient probably _____ . Also keep in
mind that children and old or infirm people are particularly vulnerable; they
are _____ , so they should always be given first priority.

Although the only cases so far have been reported outside the city, that is still
_____ for most of the county's residents. The virus could spread in any
direction, so make sure you stay informed of all cases at your local hospital. At this
point in time, we do not know how the disease spreads, so remind your patients that it
won't do them any good to _____ friends or family members who have the
disease.

Researchers are working day and night to contain the virus quickly, but as you know,
there have been similar outbreaks in the past that have become epidemics, and have
_____ . It is possible that in spite of their dedicated efforts to solve this
medical mystery, the researchers may have _____ .

However, there is no cause for alarm yet. Although it may be an _____ , the
Health Department is determined to _____ . A health official's final statement regarding this disease was, "This bug is *going* to get caught. We will not allow it
to _____ ."

II Finding the Idioms in Ads

INTERPRETING THE ADS

Look at the following advertisements. First determine what is being advertised and what idiom is featured in the ad. Review the meaning of the idiom. Then answer the questions corresponding to each ad.

1. Describe the picture. What is the minister doing?

2. Explain both the idiomatic and literal interpretations of the phrase.

1. Are the idioms in this ad used in a literal or idiomatic sense? Explain.

2. How does Old Spice help men to "save face"?

1. Is the idiom in this ad used literally or idiomatically? Explain.

2. How does the product advertised help skin irritated by a close shave?

1. Describe the picture. How does the picture relate to the line "It can keep a mountain road from becoming an uphill battle"?

2. In what way does a mountain road sometimes become an uphill battle?

3. Is the phrase "uphill battle" used in a literal or idiomatic way?

1. Describe what is happening in the picture.

2. Is the idiom used in a literal sense, an idiomatic sense, or both? Explain.

3. How does Scotchgard "stop dirt in its tracks"?

4. At the bottom of the ad, it says that this product is "Always a step ahead of a stain." What does it mean to be "a step ahead of something"?

1. America is currently very dependent on oil from foreign countries as an energy source. How does that make America a "sitting duck"?

2. What is the solution proposed by this ad?

3. How does the picture and the shape of the text contribute to the message of the ad?

THINKING ABOUT THE ADS

Review the ads from this chapter. Based on the messages contained in the ads, choose the one that you think best illustrates American cultural values. Complete statements one through four based on that ad.

1. This ad would appeal to an American audience because . . . .

2. It is important to many Americans to . . . .

3. Other examples in American life that show how Americans feel about this issue or value are . . . .

4. This ad would/would not appeal to an audience from my country because . . . .

5. The ad that I liked the best is . . . .

6. The ad that made the best use of an idiom is . . . because . . . .

III Using the Idioms

USING THE IDIOMS IN SPEECH

A. One-minute Speech

Write a brief outline before presenting your one-minute speech to your classmates. Be sure to use the idioms from this chapter in your speech.

You have been asked to speak to the legislature to convince them to enact tougher laws against people who drive their cars when they're drunk. Drunk drivers cause over half of the traffic accidents in the United States. Thousands of people are seriously injured or killed as a result of people who drink and drive. You don't believe that current laws aimed at drunk drivers are strict enough, and you would like to propose harsher and more severe punishment for those who are caught.

B. Group Discussion

Participate in the following discussion, using the idioms from this chapter.

International terrorism has become an increasingly serious problem. There is nowhere in the world where one can feel safe from the threat of violence by terrorists. Even in the United States, where most people have been somewhat insulated from terrorism, the bombing of the World Trade Center in New York City in 1993 proved that no country or its people is immune. Talk about this problem and what can be done about it with the other members of your group. Discuss the following points:

- Where do terrorist acts occur?

- Whom should we blame for terrorism?

- Is retaliatory action against a country that sponsors terrorism a legitimate response?

- What should be done with terrorists if they are caught?

- Should governments ever give in to terrorist demands?

C. Debate: Nuclear Weapons

Read the situation and choose to defend either side of the following question: Are nuclear weapons effective in maintaining world peace, or is total disarmament of nuclear weapons our only guarantee of safety? *Before you begin, jot down the arguments supporting your position. Remember to use as many of the idioms from this chapter as you can.*

Nuclear weapons have been a subject of controversy since 1945, when the first atomic bomb was detonated. Since that time, many developing nations have acquired the technology and materials necessary to manufacture nuclear weapons. The arms race is no longer between the United States and the former Soviet Union; now almost everyone has joined the race, and many people believe that the potential for world destruction is greater than ever before. Is total disarmament the answer? Or do you believe in maintaining a "balance of power"? Do nuclear weapons truly serve as a deterrent to hostile aggression? Is there any real way to "police" other countries in their attempts to manufacture nuclear weapons?

D. Role Plays

Imagine yourself in one of the situations described below. Act it out with another member of your class, using as many idioms from this chapter as you can in your conversation. You and your partner may want to write a brief script of the role play before acting it out.

1. (animal rights activist, scientist)

ANIMAL RIGHTS ACTIVIST: Hundreds of thousands of defenseless animals are killed each year in unnecessary and cruel experiments. You believe that many of these animals are exploited by unethical researchers who don't care about the suffering the animals endure. Often they are used to test cosmetics or other types of products that contribute nothing to the quality of human life. You think such experimentation should be stopped! Express your opinions.

SCIENTIST: Many people's lives have been saved by the knowledge that has come out of experimentation on animals. If new products, medicines, or surgical procedures were not first tested on animals, we could never be sure they are safe to use on humans. You and other scientists who experiment with animals are only trying to benefit humankind! Explain your stand on this issue.

2. (representative from an Indian tribe, government official)

INDIAN REPRESENTATIVE: Ever since the white settlers came, your people have always been treated very poorly. Now most of the Indians that are left live in poverty on reservations. Their housing, education, and medical care are all inferior to what other Americans have. You believe the government should help your people more.

GOVERNMENT OFFICIAL: You believe the American government has compensated the Indians very fairly for the injustices of the past. Now you think it is their responsibility to help themselves, rather than relying on government assistance. Tell the tribal representative that the Indians should no longer blame the government for their quality of life.

USING THE IDIOMS IN WRITING

E. Writing with Idioms

The story below is unfinished. How does it end? Use your imagination and finish it, either by yourself or with a partner, using many of the idioms from this chapter.

At nine o'clock on a dark, moonless night, Roger thought he saw a large black shadow pass over his window. Thinking little of it, a few minutes later he went outside to walk his dog. The night seemed quiet and peaceful, but as they strolled along, the dog appeared to tense up, his ears and tail pointing straight back and quivering nervously. Roger stopped and looked around him. "What's wrong, buddy?" he whispered to his dog. Suddenly a loud humming noise broke the calm. All around them appeared strange little creatures with heads that glowed like spooky lanterns, and Roger noticed a huge metallic sphere hovering several feet off the ground in front of him. Space aliens! The glowing creatures were moving closer and closer. Roger looked around and wondered how they would get away. At once he decided to . . . .

F. Advertising with Idioms

Make up an advertisement for any type of product not *advertised in the ads in this chapter, using one or more of the idioms you have just learned. Follow the steps listed below.*

1. Choose a product or service that you would like to advertise.

2. Determine your audience—the people most likely to buy your product or service.

3. Determine what value(s) would appeal to that audience. How are you going to incorporate that value into your ad?

4. Make up a slogan, using one of the idioms from this chapter.

5. Decide what visual cues (pictures, etc.) will accompany the slogan.

6. Write the rest of the ad.

7. Present it to the class. Do you think this ad would appeal to the other members of your class?

EFFORT

Idioms

PUT ONE'S BEST FOOT FORWARD

MAKE A SPLASH

HAVE AN EDGE

GET A LEG UP ON SOMEONE

BEND OVER BACKWARDS

STICK ONE'S NECK OUT

GO TO GREAT LENGTHS

GO TO THE ENDS OF THE EARTH

ON THE GO

TAKE SOMETHING IN STRIDE

TOE THE LINE

HAVE A GOOD HEAD ON ONE'S SHOULDERS

LET SOMEONE DOWN

I Learning the Idioms

WARMING UP

*Complete the following activities in small groups of three to five
students. Compare answers and discuss with your classmates.*

1. What characteristic is most important to success? Rank the following
   characteristics of a successful person from 1 (most important) to 4 (least
   important). Discuss your opinions with the other members of your group.

   —— ambition/determination ——————— —— intelligence

   —— creativity/talent ————————————— —— luck

2. Write the names of famous people, past or present, who have excelled in the
   following areas. Then determine which of the qualities listed above made them
   stand out in their field.

	Name	Quality
Music		
Art		
Sports		
Religion		
Politics		
Film		
Literature		
Business		
Science		

3. Discuss the following situations with the other members of your group:

   a. There are five other people applying for a job that you really want. What are you
      going to say or do in your job interview to distinguish yourself from the others?

   b. You are one of three contestants on a TV game show. A very attractive person
      of the opposite sex is behind a screen (unable to see you) asking questions to
      determine which of you three he/she would like to go out with on a date. How
      are you going to get the person to choose you?

   c. You are looking for someone to fill a highly visible and important position.
      What qualities would you expect the best applicant to demonstrate? What
      questions would you ask to find out which person is right for the job?

GETTING TO KNOW THE IDIOMS

A. Listening for Understanding

Listen to the following multiple-choice quiz, which examines what you would do in several different business situations. Consider these questions as you listen to the quiz. Afterward, discuss the answers with your classmates in pairs or small groups.

1. Have you ever gotten sick when you had an important job to do? What did you do?

2. Which do you think is harder: to supervise difficult employees or to have a difficult boss? What challenge does the mail-order business supervisor face?

3. What would you do if a less-qualified co-worker were promoted to a position that you wanted? Has that ever happened to you?

4. What is the best way to make the right impression in a business setting?

5. If an assignment at school or at work seems overwhelming, do you normally work harder to get it done, quit, or get someone to help you?

B. Identifying the Idioms

Next, read the multiple-choice quiz to which you have just listened. Throughout the quiz you will find the idioms listed below. Underline the idioms, and number them on the list in the order in which you find them. Can you tell what they mean by how they are used?

_____ put one's best foot forward   _____ toe the line

_____ let someone down   _____ on the go

_____ take something in stride   _____ have a good head on

_____ make a splash   one's shoulders

_____ bend over backwards   _____ stick one's neck out

_____ have an edge   _____ go to great lengths

_____ get a leg up on someone   _____ go to the ends of the earth

DO YOU ALWAYS PUT YOUR BEST FOOT FORWARD?

Do you have an edge in the workplace? Examine the following situations, and decide which response most closely fits what you would do.

1. You have a very important presentation to make to the board of directors of your company—one that could really advance your career. This morning, however, you woke up with a fever and a bad sore throat. You feel terrible! You should

a. put your best foot forward. Go to work anyway, and do your best in spite of how you feel.

b. call the president and tell him that you're sorry to let him down, but you won't be in because you're sick.

c. have your secretary buy donuts and coffee for the board of directors and tell them that's better than what you had planned anyway.

2. You supervise a number of employees at a mail-order business. Most of them are responsible and efficient, but one of them seems to be constantly making embarrassing mistakes. For example, one customer ordered a large man's shirt and the employee sent him a woman's bikini instead. You have tried talking to her, but she doesn't pay much attention to your instructions. You should

a. tell her that she must toe the line or lose her job. If she doesn't do what you tell her, she will be fired.

b. simply accept the fact that some people don't have a good head on their shoulders. Maybe she just needs simpler assignments.

c. call the customer, and tell him the bikini was a bonus gift for being the one-millionth customer.

3. You have gone to great lengths in your job in hopes of being promoted to manager; you come in early, stay late, and have received a lot of praise from your superiors for your exceptional work. Nevertheless, another employee (whom you consider to be less qualified) was given the position instead.

You should

a. take it in stride. Although it's disappointing, you will have other chances to get ahead.

b. sincerely congratulate the new manager on getting a leg up on you.

c. leave work early one day and flatten all the tires on the new manager's car.

4. You work for an advertising agency that is trying to get the account of a huge fast-food chain. This could mean millions of dollars for the agency; it's the chance of a lifetime! You are in charge of trying to convince the company to hire your agency. You should

a. stick your neck out by promising them that if food sales don't go up during the six months after they hire you, they won't have to pay.

b. make a splash by coming to your meeting dressed like a hamburger.

c. tell the company that you are willing to represent them only if they will change their menu; you are a vegetarian.

5. You have been working on an assignment for several weeks and the deadline for completion of your project is fast approaching. You have been staying at your office until almost ten o'clock every night, working weekends, and even taking work home to complete late at night. You are exhausted! You should

a. bend over backwards to meet the deadline. When it's all over you can take a vacation.

b. tell your boss that you've been on the go constantly for weeks and you need

some help to finish the project.

c. sweetly inform your boss that despite his perception that you would go to the ends of the earth for the company, you need your sleep more. Then go home.

Which letter did you choose most often? If you picked **a**, you definitely have an edge in the workplace. You will go to great lengths to achieve success in your career. If you picked **b** most often, you should probably work in a job that does not require a high level of responsibility. If you chose **c**, perhaps you should consider psychological counseling before applying for your next job.

C. Getting the Meaning

Notice the highlighted phrase in each of the following sentences. Pay attention to how the idiom is used, and try to guess its meaning. You may also refer to the preceding quiz. Write the meaning of the idiom on the line. The first one is done for you.

1. Scott and Mike are evenly matched in track events, but in weight lifting, Mike definitely **has an edge**.

   has an advantage

2. When Mary met Doug's parents for the first time, she **put her best foot forward**.

3. Sue's husband promised her he would stop drinking, but once again he **let her down** and got drunk.

_____

4. The rules here are very strict, so if you don't think you can **toe the line**, it would be better for you to leave now.

_____

5. Even though Joelle didn't go to college, she **has a good head on her shoulders**. You ought to listen to her.

_____

6. I'm proud of how Jeff reacted to the newspaper's review of his book. Although it was mostly negative, he just **took it in stride**.

_____

7. Barbara **got a leg up** on the other reporters by getting to the bank just after it had been robbed. She was the first one to talk to the bank manager and the police who were investigating the crime.

_____

8. Although he knew the baseball player needed a lot of work, the coach **stuck his neck out** for him and got him a chance to play with the team.

_____

9. Nicky really **made a splash** at the town meeting. A week later everyone is still talking about how great her speech was.

_____

10. That poor woman! She **bends over backwards** to make her husband happy, but he still pays more attention to other women than he does to her.

_____

11. I don't know when you even have time to eat. You are always **on the go**! Don't you ever slow down?

_____

12. Marla, believe me! I would **go to the ends of the earth** for you! What must I do to prove my everlasting love?

_____

13. Detective Barner is determined to catch the guy that killed that little boy. He will **go to great lengths** to find out who is responsible.

_____

PRACTICING THE IDIOMS

D. Choosing the Best Answer

Listen carefully to the following taped statements. Read the choices listed below for each statement you hear. Select the sentence that best relates to the original statement, and circle the corresponding letter.

1. a. Senator Curtis will probably win.
    b. Senator Curtis will have to work harder to win.

2. a. I decided to run away from my awful job.
    b. I resolved to try again and do a better job.

3. a. Everyone expected Shelly to act differently.
    b. Shelly gave us a great surprise.

4. a. Bob wants to find another job.
    b. Bob will be fired unless he does what Phyllis says.

5. a. Jim is quite good-looking.
    b. Jim is sensible and intelligent.

6. a. Joey tried to get away as soon as possible.
    b. Joey was not overly preoccupied with the earthquake.

7. a. James lost the advantage because he was too late.
    b. Billy can't go until next time.

8. a. She risks losing Calvin by forcing him to decide.
    b. It took her nine years to decide to marry Calvin.

9. a. It is probably a swimming party.
    b. You are likely to attract a lot of attention.

10. a. The extra effort didn't affect the outcome.
    b. It wasn't possible to finish on time.

11. a. Ellen had to go somewhere at six in the morning.
    b. Ellen has had a very busy day.

12. a. The professor travels all over the world to find alien beings.
    b. The professor will do anything to prove that he is correct.

13. a. Roland tried very hard to get the job.
    b. Roland had to travel far to get the job.

E. Retelling the Story—Optional Activity

Read the multiple-choice quiz on page 96–97 again. The sentences below refer to statements in that quiz. On the lines below, restate the sentences, using the appropriate idiom in each one. The first one is done for you.

1. Do you have an advantage over other workers at your job?

   Do you have an edge on the people you work with?

2. If you are sick on the day of an important presentation, you should try hard to do your best anyway.

   _____

3. Maybe you should call and tell the president you are sorry to disappoint him but you're sick.

   _____

4. When an employee doesn't pay attention or follow orders, you should tell her that if she doesn't do what is expected, you will fire her.

   _____

5. Some people are simply not very sensible.

   _____

6. If someone is promoted to a position you were hoping to fill, you should accept it and move on.

   _____

7. Should you tell the other person that you are pleased that he/she got the advantage over you?

   _____

8. If your ad agency is trying to lure a fast-food restaurant chain to be represented by you, you should take a risk and offer them free services if their sales do not improve.

   _____

9. Some people might attract attention by doing something outrageous, like dressing up as a hamburger for a meeting with representatives of a fast-food company.

   _____

10. If you are exhausted from overwork, you should do everything you can to finish the project, and then you can relax.

   _____

11. Another option is to tell your boss that you have been busy and working constantly, and you need help.

   _____

12. Your boss may believe that you would do anything for the company, but you should be more concerned with getting some sleep.

   _____

13. If you chose the letter *a* more than any other, it shows that you are willing to make a great effort to succeed in your job.

   _____

F. Putting the Idioms into Practice

You have just enrolled at Kingston University, a prestigious private university with very high standards. Your parents have written you the following letter of advice to help you during your first year. Substitute one of the idioms listed below for each of the numbered phrases. Remember to change the idioms as needed to fit the sentences.

put one's best foot forward   let someone down
take something in stride   make a splash with
bend over backwards   have an edge
get a leg up on someone   toe the line
on the go   have a good head on one's shoulders
stick one's neck out   go to great lengths
go to the ends of the earth

Dear _____,
        _{your name}

    We're so proud that you have been accepted to Kingston. I'm sure you know what a great opportunity it is to attend one of the world's finest and most prestigious universities. You _____ , and we are confident that you will be suc-
        1. are a very intelligent young person

cessful in your academic pursuits. However, we would like to offer you some advice before you begin the school year. We hope you will follow our counsel; we believe it will help you _____ the other students there.
        2. get an advantage over

You have already shown us that you are willing to _____ to do well.
<u>3. put forth a big effort</u>
That will be even more necessary in college, where you are competing against hundreds of intelligent students like yourself. You must always _____
<u>4. try your hardest and do your best</u>
in order to distinguish yourself from all the others. In fact, it probably wouldn't hurt to do something extraordinary to _____ your professors (as long as it
<u>5. attract the attention of</u>
doesn't cause you to receive any negative attention).

Be sure to always _____ while you are at the university—both in
<u>6. do what you're supposed to</u>
and out of class. You won't get anywhere if you can't follow the rules.

You may occasionally be assigned a professor who seems to be overly demanding. In such cases, you should _____ to please him or her. You might
<u>7. make an even greater effort</u>
even _____ and offer to do extra work—whatever it takes to let your profes-
<u>8. take a risk</u>
sor know that you would _____ to get a good grade. And if after all that you
<u>9. do virtually anything</u>
still get a lower mark than you expected, _____ .
<u>10. accept it and keep going</u>

If you do all these things, when you graduate you will _____ in the
<u>11. have a big advantage</u>
job market. Please don't _____ . We know that you are
<u>12. disappoint us</u>
always _____ , but we hope you will write every now and then to let us
<u>13. busy</u>
know how you're doing. We are anxious to hear about your life at Kingston.

Love always,

Mom and Dad

II Finding the Idioms in Ads

INTERPRETING THE ADS

Look at the following advertisements. First determine what is being advertised and what idiom is featured in the ad. Review the meaning of the idiom. Then answer the questions corresponding to each ad.

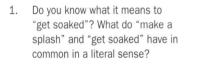

1. Do you know what it means to "get soaked"? What do "make a splash" and "get soaked" have in common in a literal sense?

2. How will the HP Paint Jet let you make a splash?

3. How will it keep you from getting soaked?

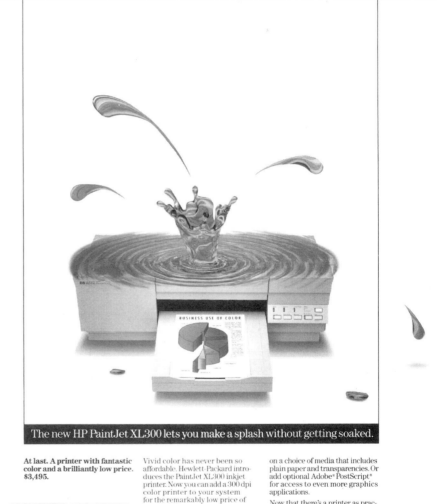

The new HP PaintJet XL300 lets you make a splash without getting soaked.

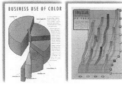

At last. A printer with fantastic color and a brilliantly low price. $3,495.

Vivid color has never been so affordable. Hewlett-Packard introduces the PaintJet XL300 inkjet printer. Now you can add a 300 dpi color printer to your system for the remarkably low price of just $3,495.*

The PaintJet XL300 has HP LaserJet printer compatibility built right in. The same typefaces. The same page formatting. It also has PC/Macintosh auto-switching, so users in a mixed environment can share. And, just like a LaserJet, the PaintJet XL300 becomes network-ready with optional HP JetDirect interface cards.

Get laser-quality text and graphics

on a choice of media that includes plain paper and transparencies. Or add optional Adobe® PostScript® for access to even more graphics applications.

Now that there's a printer as practical as the PaintJet XL300, maybe it's time you took the plunge into color. Call **1-800-752-0900, Ext. 3159** for a free print sample and the name of the authorized HP dealer nearest you.‡

HEWLETT PACKARD

Tokina goes to great lengths in auto focus lenses.

In a distinctive array of focal lengths and speeds, Tokina technology advances auto focus lenses to professional excellence at a favorable price.

Tokina auto focus lenses offer professional features including highly polished, optically proven glass. They are built for specific camera bodies: Canon, Nikon, Minolta and Pentax (no need for adapters). And they are fully compatible with all working features of today's popular auto focus cameras.

Professional Features

⊕ **Constant Aperture.** Zoom through various focal lengths (in AT-X models) without stopping to adjust f-stops.

⊕ **Sharpness at all focal lengths.** Thanks to computer-aided technology.

⊕ **Apochromatic (APO) Sharpness.** Cuts color aberations for crisp images at all focal lengths. Our AT-X lenses feature HLD (High Refractive Low Dispersion Glass) or SD (Super Low Dispersion Glass) diagrammed here.

New AF Wide Angle

20-35 f/3.5–4.5. Ideal for landscapes and family portraits. HLD glass. 2.7" long. 16.2 oz.

You can pay a lot more for a lens, but money won't make it better than Tokina.

AT-X AF 400 to be available shortly.

TOKINA AT-X AF SERIES

28-70 f/2.8. Lens of the Year in Japan. Constant aperture. HLD glass. 3.7" long. 20.8 oz.
80-200 f/2.8. Professional favorite the world over. Constant aperture. SD glass. 7.0" long. 41.6 oz.
300mm f/2.8. Sports, action favorite SD glass. 8.5" long. 68.4 oz.
400mm f/5.6. For wildlife and sports photography. SD glass. 8.1" long. 36 oz.

Steve Gilroy is an internationally recognized outdoor and travel photographer. He took this photo on the Bio Bio River in Chile with the 80-200 f/2.6

SD APOCHROMATIC LENSES   HLD

ⓣTokina®
FOREMOST IN INNOVATIVE LENS TECHNOLOGY

No charge for 5 year warranty. (10 year warranty on AT-X professional lenses.) For information and nearest Tokina dealer call (800)-421-1141 (Outside CA) or (213) 537-9380. Tokina Optical Corporation, 1512 Kona Drive, Compton, CA 90220.

Circle No. 53 on Reader Service Card

1. What does a camera lens do?

2. There is a literal as well as an idiomatic meaning to the statement, "Tokina goes to great lengths in auto focus lenses." Can you explain both meanings?

JOSÉ IS A VIRTUOSO AT ENSURING YOU ALWAYS PUT YOUR BEST FOOT FORWARD.

At Four Seasons Hotels, we know that brilliantly shined shoes can reflect positively on those who wear them. Thus, our valets will unfailingly polish your Oxfords and pumps to mirror-like perfection, make small repairs, if needed, then return the shoes with dispatch to their rightful destination. And not only is the shoeshine worthy of compliments, but at Four Seasons it's always complimentary. Which fits comfortably with our belief that in these value-conscious times, the demands of your trip should demand nothing less than Four Seasons Hotels.

Four Seasons Hotels·Resorts

1. What is José's job?

2. How does José help you put your best foot forward?

3. Is the idiom in this ad used literally, idiomatically, or both? Explain.

1. The picture shows a pocket knife with a large variety of instruments. What are these meant to represent?

2. How does the picture relate to the statement, "We have the edge you need to meet any financial challenge"?

1. What does "pull for" mean?

2. How does VISA help you pull for the U.S. Olympic team?

3. How does the idiom "bend over backwards" relate to the picture?

1. Who is featured in the picture? What is he doing?

2. What does "stride" mean? How does the idiom "Take obstacles in stride" relate to the picture?

3. There is another idiom in the small text of this ad: "To clear any hurdle." what do you think this means? How does that idiom relate to the picture?

THINKING ABOUT THE ADS

Review the ads from this chapter. Based on the messages contained in the ads, choose the one that you think best illustrates American cultural values. Complete one through four statements based on that ad.

1. This ad would appeal to an American audience because . . . .

2. It is important to many Americans to . . . .

3. Other examples in American life that show how Americans feel about this issue or value are . . . .

4. This ad would/would not appeal to an audience from my country because . . . .

5. The ad that I liked the best is . . . .

6. The ad that made the best use of an idiom is . . . because . . . .

III Using the Idioms

USING THE IDIOMS IN SPEECH

A. One-minute Speech

Write a brief outline before presenting your one-minute speech to your classmates. Be sure to use the idioms from this chapter in your speech.

You are a drama coach for several young actors and actresses (played by the other members of your group). They are about to audition for their first big part in a movie. What should they do to get the part? What advice can you give them to increase their chances of the director choosing them? Give them a "pep talk" to encourage and motivate them to do their best.

B. Group Discussion

Participate in the following discussion, using the idioms from this chapter.

You are all members of a special public relations group that has been hired to help out a candidate for vice president of the United States. The candidate, Bob Bore, is highly respected in political circles, but the public perceives him as being too stiff and lacking good personal communication skills. Your job is to help him change his image so that the public will see him as warm, friendly, and concerned. Discuss the following:

- The candidate is always running on a very tight schedule. Should he slow down and take more time to talk to individuals?

- Mr. Bore needs to make a good impression on each new group he meets; maybe he should take more risks and do extraordinary things to get people's attention.

- The American public needs to see his strong points: He is highly intelligent and will do what is required to get things done.

- People should feel that he would do absolutely anything for his country and that he won't disappoint them.

- How can Mr. Bore gain an advantage over his opponent?

C. Debate: Grading on a Curve

Read the situation and choose to defend either side of the following question: Is the system of grading on a curve fair to all students? *Before you begin, jot down the arguments supporting your position. Remember to use as many of the idioms from this chapter as you can.*

Many students in schools around the United States are doomed to failure because of the time-honored system of grading on a curve. In classes where teachers use this traditional method of determining the grades in a class, a certain number of students will fail. On most exams, the scores typically fall into a *bell curve* pattern: There are a few outstanding scores, a lot of average scores, and a few low scores. No matter how high the low scores are, if the teacher grades on a curve, they fail because they are below the average. It can be argued, of course, that anyone can avoid being below average, and that the system does an excellent job of eliminating those who probably shouldn't be there in the first place. On the other hand, because the curve shifts a little to the right or to the left with different groups of students, the definition of average changes as well. What was a high mark in one class may be a low mark in another, and vice versa. Is this system fair?

D. Role Plays

Imagine yourself in one of the situations described below. Act it out with another member of your class, using as many idioms from this chapter as you can in your conversation. You and your partner may want to write a brief script of the role play before acting it out.

1. (hypnotist, client)

HYPNOTIST: Your client is a heavy smoker. He/she has tried to quit on several occasions, but nothing has worked so far. Tell your client that you can guarantee that your treatment works: Your client *will* stop if he/she really wants to. Convince your client that it is worth the effort to quit.

CLIENT: You really want to stop smoking, and you would do just about anything to succeed this time. Tell the hypnotist that you will do whatever is required of you.

2. (unemployed worker, job counselor)

WORKER: You have been out of work for about a year, and during that time you have lost all confidence in your ability to get a job. Although you are intelligent, you don't know how to make the right impression on a prospective employer.

COUNSELOR: You need to instruct this worker on various techniques that would help him/her get a good job. Help this person understand what is required of a good employee, and what a prospective employer will look for.

USING THE IDIOMS IN WRITING

E. Writing with Idioms

Retell the story described below, using the idioms from this chapter.

Do you know the story of "The Tortoise and the Hare?" The tortoise (turtle) and the hare (rabbit) run a race, which the hare is naturally expected to win. However, after taking a huge lead, the overconfident hare stops to take a nap, and as he sleeps, the slow but persistent tortoise passes him and wins the race. Can you retell this story, or any other popular fable in which the characters of the story make an extraordinary effort to succeed?

F. Advertising with Idioms

Make up an advertisement for any type of product not *advertised in the ads in this chapter, using one or more of the idioms you have just learned. Follow the steps listed below.*

1. Choose a product or service that you would like to advertise.

2. Determine your audience—the people most likely to buy your product or service.

3. Determine what value(s) would appeal to that audience. How are you going to incorporate that value into your ad?

4. Make up a slogan, using one of the idioms from this chapter.

5. Decide what visual cues (pictures, etc.) will accompany the slogan.

6. Write the rest of the ad.

7. Present it to the class. Do you think this ad would appeal to the other members of your class?

7

AMBITION

Idioms

CORPORATE LADDER

FAST TRACK

TOP BANANA

CALL THE SHOTS

TAKE THE HEAT

KEEP UP WITH THE TIMES

MAKE SOMETHING FLY

HAVE A NOSE FOR SOMETHING

MEAN BUSINESS

FEATHER ONE'S NEST

NEST EGG

FOLLOW IN SOMEONE'S FOOTSTEPS

OPEN DOORS

CAN YOUR ANTI-PERSPIRANT TAKE THE HEAT?

DEGREE CAN. IT'S BODY-HEAT ACTIVATED.

Only *DEGREE* has the Body-Heat Activated formula that releases extra protection when you really need it. *DEGREE.® YOUR BODY HEAT TURNS IT ON.*

I Learning the Idioms

WARMING UP

*First fill in the following grid yourself by marking in the appropriate
column whether you would, at first thought, imagine a man or a
woman in the following professions. (Be honest!) Then poll two to
four of your classmates (both men and women, if possible), and mark
their answers. Are you surprised by the results?*

	Man	**Woman**
doctor		
teacher		
writer		
firefighter		
photographer		
lawyer		
politician		
chef		
flight attendant		
artist		
professional athlete		

*In small groups of three to five students, discuss the following questions. Compare
answers and discuss with your classmates.*

1. Explain what your reaction would be:

   a. After the airplane you are in takes off, the pilot gets on the loudspeaker to
      welcome the passengers aboard. You realize the pilot is a woman.

   b. You have just been hired to work at a large company. On your first day at your
      new job, a middle-aged man comes into your office and asks if you have any
      work for him to do. You don't understand what he means until he announces,
      "I'm your new secretary."

2. Why do you think most men work: to earn money, to find self-fulfillment, or to do
   their duty as members of society? Why do you think most women work?

3. Are there any jobs that you think men do better than women? Are there any jobs
   that you think a woman could not or should not do? Are there any jobs that you
   think a man could not or should not do?

Getting to Know the Idioms

A. Listening for Understanding

Listen to the following interview between a magazine journalist and the top manager of a large company. Consider these questions as you listen to the interview. Afterward, discuss the answers with your classmates in pairs or small groups.

1. Why did *Women's Work* interview Cheryl Dobbs?

2. Why was Cheryl Dobbs successful in business? Was being a woman an advantage or a disadvantage?

3. What does Ms. Dobbs plan to do for women at Astrotech Industries?

4. Do you think that the men working at Astrotech are at a disadvantage in any way? Explain.

5. Is it common for women to be in management positions in your country? Where you come from, is it more difficult for women to get ahead in business than it is for men? Compare the role of women in business in the United States to that of businesswomen in your country.

6. Are there any jobs in your country that would not be available to women? Are there any jobs that would not be available to men? Why?

B. Identifying the Idioms

Next, read the interview to which you have just listened.
Throughout the interview you will find the idioms listed below.
Underline the idioms, and number them on the list in the order in
which you find them. Can you tell what they mean by how they are
used?

_____ **feather one's nest**   _____ **call the shots**

_____ **take the heat**   _____ **corporate ladder**

_____ **keep up with the times**   _____ **nest egg**

_____ **fast track**   _____ **open doors**

_____ **mean business**   _____ **follow in someone's footsteps**

_____ **top banana**   _____ **have a nose for something**

_____ **make something fly**

CLIMBING THE CORPORATE LADDER

Women's Work magazine is a monthly periodical that deals with women's issues, particularly as they relate to business. Cheryl Dobbs, a business-woman who was recently appointed as president of Astrotech Industries, was featured on the cover of the most recent issue of *Women's Work*. The following is an excerpt from the magazine's interview with Ms. Dobbs.

Women's Work: Congratulations! I'm certain that I speak for most of the women of America when I say how proud we are of you and your accomplishments. How does it feel to be the top banana of one of the most successful companies in the United States?

Cheryl Dobbs: Thank you. Right now I feel very lucky, but that doesn't mean I don't appreciate the challenges of managing a billion-dollar corporation. Everything is going well now, but I'm sure that soon I'll have to take the heat for any problems we may encounter. In addition, the company is just starting some big new projects, and I've got to make them fly in order to prove myself. I'm sure it won't be an easy job.

Women's Work: Cheryl, a lot of people were surprised by your appointment because no woman has ever held such a high position at Astrotech Industries. Do you feel that being a woman helped or hurt you on your way up the corporate ladder?

Cheryl Dobbs: Actually, I think it did both. It is undeniable that being a woman kept me off the fast track during the early days of my career. Women simply were not expected to be promoted to management positions. But even though it probably took me longer than many male executives, I proved that I could be effective. It seems I have a nose for good investment and expansion opportunities—every deal I proposed helped the company grow and prosper, and perhaps because I am a woman, my accomplishments were noticed more easily than those of some of my male colleagues. Consequently, I think I have helped to open doors for a lot of other women in business. It may not be quite so tough now for them to get ahead.

Women's Work: Now that you are calling the shots, do you plan to change anything at Astrotech in order to make top management positions more accessible to women?

Cheryl Dobbs: Yes. Like all progressive companies, we need to keep up with the times, and that includes providing women with opportunities to move into positions that were previously closed to them. A lot of women today are very serious about their careers; when they go to work, they mean business. A fulfilling career means as much to them as it traditionally has to men. Furthermore, we must be sure that we are giving women financial compensation equal to their male counterparts. There are now more women than ever who can't be, or don't want to be, financially dependent on a man. Women are often the principal providers for themselves and their families, so it's up to them to feather their nest. And, of course, women are concerned about their retirement also—they want to build up a good-sized nest egg now for when they can no longer work. That means they can no longer be content to be just secretaries. They want more from their jobs—emotionally and financially. We're definitely going to see more and more female executives in corporate boardrooms, at least here at Astrotech.

Women's Work: Well, Cheryl, you are a terrific role model for women everywhere, as well as for men. I'm sure that anyone in the business world would be honored to follow in your footsteps. Good luck to you and to Astrotech.

C. Getting the Meaning

Notice the highlighted phrase in each of the following sentences. Pay attention to how the idiom is used, and try to guess its meaning. You may also refer to the preceding interview. Write the meaning of the idiom on the line. The first one is done for you.

1. It's hard to believe that Clark started out as a messenger in the mail room. Now he's the **top banana**!

    the person in charge; the head of the organization

2. Although the airplane crash was blamed on a terrorist act, the airline is **taking the heat** for having inadequate security.

3. Sherry came up with a great plan to increase awareness of our global resources. I just hope she can **make it fly**.

4. Steve spent a lot of time in a boring desk job, but once the boss noticed him, he started moving up the **corporate ladder** pretty fast.

5. Peter must be on the **fast track** in the company he works for now. He's been promoted three times in the last year.

6. I really didn't study much for that test; I just **have a nose for** the right answers.

7. The new scholarship fund will **open doors** for a lot of students who otherwise would not have been able to go to college.

8. If you don't agree with my decisions, you can quit. Remember, I'm **calling the shots** now.

9. My manual typewriter still works fine, but to **keep up with the times**, I'm going to have to buy a computer.

10. Mr. Gray called me this morning with an offer that is much higher than any others we've received, and he said he's ready to pay cash. Apparently, he **means business**.

_____

11. It took me twenty-five years to **feather my nest**, and only two hours for the fire to destroy everything!

_____

12. My parents worked their entire lives to build up a good-sized **nest egg**. Now that they're retired, they can finally do all the things they could never afford before.

_____

13. Jackie **followed in her father's footsteps**. She became a lawyer, like him, and even took over his law practice when he retired.

_____

PRACTICING THE IDIOMS

D. Choosing the Best Answer

Listen carefully to the following taped statements. Decide if the sentence that corresponds to each is true or false. Circle T if it is true and F if it is false.

1. T / F   I insist upon speaking to the person in charge.

2. T / F   This nation's problems are the president's fault.

3. T / F   Whoever is responsible for the food should deliver it by airplane so it will arrive in time for lunch.

4. T / F   Joe doesn't care much about business.

5. T / F   Impressing your boss should improve your chances of being promoted.

6. T / F   Bruce always smells the coins before he buys them.

7. T / F   Maria's job involves opening and closing the doors of the business as clients walk in and out.

8. T / F   They both seem to be fighting for control in their relationship.

9.   T / F   Ice cream isn't as popular as it once was.

10. T /F   Jared is more seriously committed to his current girlfriend than he has been to previous ones.

11. T / F   I have a more limited budget than you do.

12. T / F   The mine collapsed on top of her nest egg.

13. T / F   Joey didn't want to live very close to his brother.

E. Retelling the Story—Optional Activity

Read the interview on page 114–115 again. The sentences below refer to statements in that interview. On the lines below, restate the sentences, using the appropriate idiom in each one. The first one is done for you.

1. Cheryl Dobbs is now the head of Astrotech Industries.

    Cheryl Dobbs is the top banana at Astrotech Industries.

2. Although things are running smoothly now, when problems come up, Ms. Dobbs will have to deal with the pressure and the criticism.

    _____

3. Astrotech is starting to work on some new projects, and it is Ms. Dobbs's responsibility to make them work.

    _____

4. Being a woman was an advantage as well as a disadvantage as Ms. Dobbs was promoted through the ranks of the company.

    _____

5. At first, she was not promoted very fast or regularly.

    _____

6. Later on, however, people noticed Ms. Dobbs because she has an innate sense for making good deals.

    _____

7. Because of her success and high visibility, she has increased the opportunities for other women to get ahead.

_____

8. Now that she is in charge, Ms. Dobbs is planning on changing some things at Astrotech.

_____

9. She realizes the need to be modern and up-to-date in company policies and practices.

_____

10. She also recognizes that when many women enter a profession, they are very serious about their careers.

_____

11. Many women are financially responsible for providing many of the material comforts of their homes.

_____

12. Women also want to save up money for when they stop working or retire.

_____

13. Cheryl Dobbs's success is likely to inspire many other people in business to follow her example.

_____

F. Putting the Idioms into Practice

Read the following news article. Then answer the questions following the article, using the idioms shown in parentheses in your answers.

BROTHERS CHARGED IN PARENTS' DEATHS

The entertainment industry was rocked today by the news of the execution-style murders of Pablo and Cindy Mayorga outside their home in Beverly Hills. An even greater shock, however, came later in the day when the Mayorga's two sons were arrested and charged with the deaths of their parents. Although both young men are suspected of planning the grisly act, Joe, at twenty years the older of the two, will probably face a more serious charge, since his seventeen-year-old younger brother is a minor.

Pablo Mayorga, the head of Hollyville Entertainment, was credited with putting together a string of movie hits unmatched by any other production company. He had won the respect and admiration of the entire industry, having proven to his greatest competitors that he was seriously committed to being the best.

After quickly and successfully working his way up at Tower Pictures, Mr. Mayorga established his own production company, Hollyville Entertainment, so he could be completely in charge. Although he had never before been in business for himself, Mr. Mayorga took repeated risks early on by developing new projects that no other company wanted, and to everyone's surprise, making them work. He was reportedly a strict and demanding employer who nevertheless provided opportunities for many minorities, like himself, to rise quickly in the business. He often spent large amounts of money to make sure that his company reflected modern trends. He was perhaps best known for having an inbred sense for knowing which movies would be popular with the public and which would not.

Although Mr. Mayorga was also known as a man who always made sure his family lived in luxurious comfort, he was apparently not on good terms with his sons. According to a neighbor, the two young men often argued bitterly with their father over his desire for them to take the same career path that he had followed. Friends of the family have also suggested that perhaps the sons were impatient to collect the huge financial savings that they were due to inherit after their parents' death. However, if the young men are convicted, they may wait an even longer time to spend the money; the minimum sentence for which they could qualify is life in prison.

1. Who was Pablo Mayorga? (top banana)

   _____

2. Who is likely to face the more serious charge for the murders, and why? (take the heat)

   _____

3. How did Mr. Mayorga earn the respect and admiration of the entertainment industry? (mean business)

   _____

4. How would you describe Mr. Mayorga's employment at Tower Pictures? (fast track/corporate ladder)

_____

5. Why did Mr. Mayorga establish his own production company? (call the shots)

_____

6. What did Mr. Mayorga do soon after going into business for himself that was surprising to many of his competitors? (make something fly)

_____

7. What did he do for minorities in his organization? (open doors)

_____

8. Why did he often spend a lot of money on his business? (keep up with the times)

_____

9. What was he best known for? (have a nose for something)

_____

10. In what conditions did the Mayorga family live, and why? (feather one's nest)

_____

11. Why did the two sons argue with their father? (follow in one's footsteps)

_____

12. What were the young men hoping to get after their parents' deaths? (nest egg)

_____

II Finding the Idioms in Ads

INTERPRETING THE ADS

Look at the following advertisements. First determine what is being advertised and what idiom is featured in the ad. Review the meaning of the idiom. Then answer the questions corresponding to each ad.

1. What is this Samsonite product used for?

2. What do they compare their garment bag to? Why?

3. Is the idiom in this ad used in a literal or idiomatic way? Explain.

1. When you are driving, what is the function of the passing lane? How does the idea of a passing lane fit in with the idiom in this ad?

2. How would reading the *Wall Street Journal* help you in your business career?

1. Who was Cyrano? What was he known for?

2. Can you explain the line "But I definitely have a nose for birthday gifts"?

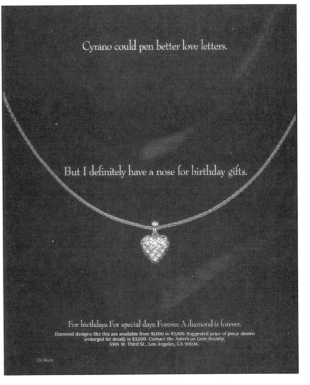

1. *Prefab* is short for prefabricated. What do "Prefab," "Ready-made," and "Throw-away" refer to?

2. In what way has Albert Wittnauer not kept up with the times? Is that an advantage or a disadvantage? Why?

With our risk management expertise, we can make your nest egg look like it came from an ostrich.

It's something that's been drilled into your head for years: to really make your money grow, you have to be willing to accept a lot of risk.

An axiom of investment, right? Self-evident. Incontestable. Or is it?

At Continental Bank, we're not so sure. Why continue to assume risk, we'd like to know, when there are so many effective ways to manage it?

After all, you're not in the investment game simply to minimize

Hummingbird egg (actual size)   *Cuckoo egg (actual size)*   *Tern egg (actual size)*   *Chicken egg (actual size)*

your risk, you're in it to maximize your return. To beat the bogey, as they say.

What you need, then, is a bank that can actually help you capitalize on economic change. A bank for whom opportunism has become, over time, expected behavior. A bank that looks not only to beat the bogey, but to score the financial equivalent of a hole-in-one.

A bank, more specifically, whose logo happens to be located in the bottom right-hand corner of the adjacent page.

For the people at Continental, after all, outperforming the industry is not the exception. It's the rule. Because when we do our financial homework, we're conscientious enough to explore each and every investment option.

"Options, swaptions," you say with still a trace of skepticism? Ironic that you should, because you've just named two of our most commonly used risk management tools, tools which not only include

Gull egg (actual size)   *Ostrich egg (actual size)*

options and swaptions, but caps, collars, swaps, forwards and futures.

Speaking of futures, why not begin insuring yours by calling Continental at (312) 828-3155? Rest assured, we'll protect you from financial risk. But when the right opportunity comes along, we won't be caught with our head in the sand.

Ⓒ Continental Bank
A new approach to business.

---

1. What bird lays the largest egg?

2. What message is Continental Bank trying to convey to potential customers? Why would you want to put your nest egg there?

1. Where do you think this man is going? Does he look relaxed? Describe how he might be feeling.

2. This idiom is being used in both a literal and an idiomatic sense. When you are nervous, anxious, or in a hurry, what happens to your body temperature?

THINKING ABOUT THE ADS

Review the ads from this chapter. Based on the messages contained in the ads, choose the one that you think best illustrates American cultural values. Complete statements one through four based on that ad.

1. This ad would appeal to an American audience because . . . .

2. It is important to many Americans to . . . .

3. Other examples in American life that show how Americans feel about this issue or value are . . . .

4. This ad would/would not appeal to an audience from my country because . . . .

5. The idiom that I liked best is . . . .

6. The idiom that made the best use of an idiom is . . . because . . . .

III Using the Idioms

USING THE IDIOMS IN SPEECH

A. One-minute Speech

Write a brief outline before presenting your one-minute speech to your classmates. Be sure to use the idioms from this chapter in your speech.

You have owned and operated your own business very successfully for over twenty years. Recently, you were asked to speak to a group of young entrepreneurs who are interested in starting their own independent businesses about the advantages and disadvantages of being your own boss and managing your own business. What can you tell them?

B. Group Discussion

Participate in the following discussion, using the idioms from this chapter.

There are certain characteristics that an employer looks for in the people interviewed for a job, while the prospective employee considers other factors related to the job. The following questions reflect some of the issues that both the boss and the employee might think about. Discuss which items might be most important.

The boss might think about

1. How will the prospective employee handle the pressure when things go wrong?

2. Is this person serious about fulfilling the demands of the job?

3. Does the person seem to have an instinctual sense of how the job should be done?

4. Will he/she remain up-to-date with the latest skills or technology required to do the job?

The prospective employee might think about

1. Will the job pay enough to allow me to buy things to make my home comfortable, as well as to save up for retirement?

2. Does it appear that I will be able to move up quickly in the business?

3. Will this job provide me with better professional opportunities later on?

4. Will I be in charge?

C. Debate: The Police Chief

Read the situation and choose to defend either side of the following question: Should the woman win her lawsuit against the city? *Before you begin, jot down the arguments supporting your position. Remember to use as many of the idioms from this chapter as you can.*

In a large midwestern city, a woman was promoted to the office of chief of police. However, although she was clearly more qualified than any of the top-ranking men in the department, most of the members of the largely male police force went on strike to protest her appointment. They contended that they could not accept or support a woman as chief of police. The strike continued even when riots in the city broke out, compromising the safety of the residents. Finally, the city council agreed to appoint a man instead and offered the woman a different job in the department. The woman, angry and humiliated over what she perceived as gender discrimination, sued the city and the police department for $750,000—the amount of money she would have earned if she had been allowed to serve as police chief for ten years.

D. Role Plays

Imagine yourself in one of the situations described below. Act it out with another member of your class, using as many idioms from this chapter as you can in your conversation. You and your partner may want to write a brief script of the role play before acting it out.

1. (student, friend)

STUDENT: You are enrolled in a business administration program at a prestigious university. You are also married and have two children. Your family depends on you to support them, so in addition to going to school full time, you are working at night. You still have one year to go in the program, and you have decided to drop out of school. It is much too difficult to study, work, and maintain a good relationship with your family as well.

FRIEND: Your friend is thinking about quitting school to work full time. You are certain this is a mistake, as your friend can never be as successful in his profession as he would be if he completed the program. Try to convince him to stay for the last year.

2. (newspaper reporter, Donald Trump's secretary)

REPORTER: You have been assigned to interview Donald Trump (a rich and successful American businessman). What are you going to ask him?

TRUMP'S SECRETARY: Your boss was supposed to meet with a newspaper reporter, but at the last minute he said he was too busy, and asked you to do the interview for him.

Using the Idioms in Writing

E. Writing with Idioms

Write a letter based on the situation described below, using the idioms from this chapter.

Business World magazine has a special column called "How to Get Ahead in Business." Every month they publish letters from their readers with advice on handling various issues in the business world. This month they are asking readers to offer advice on the topics listed below. Choose one, and write a letter to *Business World* with your recommendations.

- How to be an effective and popular boss.

- How to make sure you get that promotion you've been hoping for.

- Financial advice for the twenty-first century.

F. Advertising with Idioms

Make up an advertisement for any type of product not *advertised in the ads in this chapter, using one or more of the idioms you have just learned. Follow the steps listed below.*

1. Choose a product or service that you would like to advertise.

2. Determine your audience—the people most likely to buy your product or service.

3. Determine what value(s) would appeal to that audience. How are you going to incorporate that value into your ad?

4. Make up a slogan, using one of the idioms from this chapter.

5. Decide what visual cues (pictures, etc.) will accompany the slogan.

6. Write the rest of the ad.

7. Present it to the class. Do you think this ad would appeal to the other members of your class?

Idioms

TAKE IT EASY

LIVE IT UP

HAVE A BLAST

PAINT THE TOWN RED

MAKE ONE'S DAY

CATCH ONE'S EYE

TAKE ONE'S BREATH AWAY

TOP-OF-THE-LINE

DRESSED TO KILL

KEEP UP WITH THE JONESES

BENEATH ONE

AT ONE'S FEET

ON THE HOUSE

I Learning the Idioms

WARMING UP

If you could plan the vacation of your dreams, where would you go? What would you do? Complete the following grid by checking your vacation preferences, and then survey three to five of your classmates to see what they would like best. Keep track of their responses. What type of vacation is most popular?

Would You Prefer To:	You				
go to a busy metropolitan city go to a quiet, remote area					
go camping stay in a hotel					
go someplace hot and tropical go someplace cold and mountainous					
go with a tour group plan your own itinerary					
be physically active and busy just rest and relax					

Complete the following activity in small groups.

Imagine that you and your classmates work for a travel agency. Business is slow, so your manager has decided to give a bonus to the group of agents who sell the most vacation packages this month. In groups of three or four, plan a "dream vacation," one which you believe will attract the most customers. Discuss the elements listed below. *NOTE:* The vacations should last one week and should all cost the same amount.

1. The mode of transportation used to get to the vacation spot.
2. The accommodations for the travelers.
3. The location (island, mountains, city, etc). You may name a specific location if you want.
4. The schedule and type of activities planned.
5. Anything else that makes your vacation special.

After you have planned your perfect vacation, choose a spokesperson from your group to "sell" it to the rest of the class. When all "travel agents" have described their vacations, vote on the vacation you would most like to take. (You may *not* vote for your agency's vacation.) Which vacation was the most popular? Why?

GETTING TO KNOW THE IDIOMS

A. Listening for Understanding

Listen to the following advertisement for a tropical resort. Consider these questions as you listen to the advertisement. Afterward, discuss the answers with your classmates in pairs or small groups.

1. Who is the intended audience for this advertisement for the Laguna de Oro Resort?

2. How does the Laguna de Oro entice its guests to come and stay there?

3. What does the resort have to offer once the guests arrive?

4. What are some of the things the former guests especially liked about the resort?

5. Do you think you would enjoy a stay at the Laguna de Oro? Why or why not?

B. Identifying the Idioms

Next, read the advertisement to which you have just listened. Throughout this ad you will find the idioms listed below. Underline the idioms, and number them on the list in the order in which you find them. Can you tell what they mean by how they are used?

_____ paint the town red   _____ live it up

_____ right at one's feet   _____ take one's breath away

_____ have a blast   _____ take it easy

_____ top-of-the-line   _____ on the house

_____ make one's day   _____ catch one's eye

_____ dressed to kill   _____ beneath one

_____ keep up with the Joneses

Take It Easy!

Are you tired of business meetings, telephones ringing, heartburn and indigestion? Do you wish you could forget about deadlines, appointments, schedules, and late hours? Have you had enough of headaches, bills to pay, and keeping up with the Joneses? Don't you think you need to take it easy?

Sit back for a moment and imagine warm, Caribbean breezes . . . white beaches covered with sand as fine as powder, lined with gently swaying palm trees . . . golf, tennis, swimming, windsurfing, waterskiing . . . brilliant tropical sunsets that will take your breath away . . . all the comforts of a top-of-the-line resort right at your feet . . .

Aaaaaaahhh . . . now don't you feel better? Are you ready for a vacation yet?

Call your travel agent now, and make your reservations for the *Laguna de Oro* resort. We're waiting just for you, here at one of the most fabulous island resorts in the world. The Traveler's Guide gives it five stars, and Global Visions magazine said, "If ordinary hotels are beneath you, you ought to try a week at the elegant *Laguna de Oro* resort. It will be the most unforgettable week of your life!"

From the moment you arrive at the airport, we will do everything we can to make your day. We promise to treat you like royalty, beginning with your ride in one of our luxurious limousines. Once you get to *Laguna de Oro*, you can relax and let us take care of everything. Walk along the beach, play a round of golf, eat at one of our six award-winning restaurants, or just lounge by the pool. Whatever you choose, we guarantee your satisfaction.

This is what some of our thousands of satisfied and rejuvenated customers have said about their experience at our resort:

Ray and Bonita Mendel, Richmond, Virginia: "We had a blast! Every day we went windsurfing, snorkeling, or sailing. Our stay couldn't have been better!"

Chad Merrill, Los Angeles, California: "I met a beautiful woman at dinner one night. She was dressed to kill and caught my eye immediately. The rest of the week we had a wonderful time. On my last night there, we reserved a limousine for the evening and really painted the town red. I've never had so much fun!"

Rebecca Wagner, Portland, Oregon: "I tell all my friends about my perfect vacation at the Laguna de Oro resort. It was just like a dream come true! If you really want to live it up, don't miss this fabulous resort!"

Aren't you ready for that vacation yet? Don't delay! Call now, and if you reserve one full week at the *Laguna de Oro* resort, your last night's stay is on the house!

C. Getting the Meaning

*Notice the highlighted phrase in each of the following sentences.
Pay attention to how the idiom is used, and try to guess its
meaning. You may also refer to the preceding advertisement. Write
the meaning of the idiom on the line. The first one is done for you.*

1. Judy's always worried that her neighbors are going to drive up in a nicer car than hers. She spends all her money just trying to **keep up with the Joneses**.

   to compete with one's neighbors in obtaining material goods

2. Don't worry about the deadlines you have to meet at work next week. It's Saturday—**take it easy**!

3. The size and capacity of the new nuclear plant will **take your breath away**.

4. I'll have a salesman show you our **top-of-the-line** computer. There is no other model that is as good as this one.

5. When my grandfather came to America, he felt that the government had put every opportunity to succeed **right at his feet**.

6. Wouldn't you rather take a limousine? Riding in a taxi is **beneath you**!

7. I saw an old friend who said I looked as young as I did when we were in college. She **made my day**!

8. The kids **had a blast** at Disneyland! What a fun place!

9. It must be a very special event that Bob is taking you to tonight. You're **dressed to kill**!

   DRESS

10. As I was walking through a small art gallery, this painting **caught my eye** immediately.

   _____ TO ▷ _____

11. On my last night in New York City, I decided to go out with a group of my friends and **paint the town red**. I'd never had so much fun!

   _____

12. Although Mr. Daniels is retiring next year, don't expect him to stay at home and watch TV. He's worked hard all his life, and now he wants to **live it up**.

   _____

13. You don't have to pay for your first drink; it's **on the house**.

   _____

PRACTICING THE IDIOMS

D. Choosing the Best Answer

Listen carefully to the following taped statements. Read the choices listed below for each statement you hear. Select the sentence that best relates to the original statement, and circle the corresponding letter.

1. a. You must keep up with the Joneses.
    b. It caught my eye.
    c. It is beneath you.

2. a. It's right at their feet.
    b. The game is on the house.
    c. It would make my day.

3. a. They're dressed to kill.
    b. They take my breath away.
    c. They're living it up.

4. a. They had a blast.
    b. They were dressed to kill.
    c. They painted the town red.

5. a. He takes it easy.
    b. It's top-of-the-line.
    c. It's beneath him.

6. a. Let's paint the town red!
    b. Let's keep up with the Joneses!
    c. They are top-of-the-line.

7. a. It's on the house.
    b. It will catch your eye.
    c. It's all right at your feet.

8. a. It was top-of-the-line.
    b. I painted the town red.
    c. It took my breath away.

9. a. They must be living it up.
    b. It must be on the house.
    c. It's a blast.

10. a. I took it easy.
    b. It made my day.
    c. I was trying to keep up with the Joneses.

11. a. She was right at your feet.
    b. She was dressed to kill!
    c. She was top-of-the-line.

12. a. He made my day.
    b. He's trying to keep up with the Joneses.
    c. He was living it up.

13. a. It's beneath her.
    b. It's on the house.
    c. It takes her breath away.

E. Retelling the Story—Optional Activity

Read the advertisement on page 132–133 again. The sentences below refer to statements in that ad. On the lines below, restate the sentences, using the appropriate idiom in each one. The first one is done for you.

1. Are you tired of getting headaches, paying your bills, and trying to compete with the rest of the world?

    Have you had enough of headaches, bills, and keeping up with the Joneses?

2. Shouldn't you relax?

    _____

3. Imagine a place that will amaze you with its beauty.

_____

4. We can offer you all of the advantages of the very finest resorts.

_____

5. All of the comforts of the resort will be readily available to you.

_____

6. A magazine said that if common hotels are not good enough for you, perhaps you should stay at the Laguna de Oro.

_____

7. Everyone at the resort will try his/her best to make you happy.

_____

8. Two satisfied guests wrote to say they had a lot of fun at the Laguna de Oro resort.

_____

9. Another guest told of a woman he had met who was fabulously dressed.

_____

10. The woman attracted his attention right away.

_____

11. One evening, the man and the woman had a good time going to clubs and restaurants in town.

_____

12. Another guest had told all her friends to go to the Laguna de Oro if they wanted to enjoy themselves to the fullest.

_____

13. If you reserve one whole week at the resort, your last night is free!

_____

F. Putting the Idioms into Practice

You work for the Travel and Tourist Information Bureau for the city of Mountaincrest, a relatively small mountain village that subsists mostly on its tourist industry. Travelers to the area often call your office to ask for suggestions or advice on any of the attractions your city offers. In one day, you answered the following phone calls and responded to the callers' questions. Rephrase each answer by substituting one of the idioms below for the highlighted phrase. Change the idioms as needed to correctly answer the question.

catch one's eye	**dressed to kill**
paint the town red	**keep up with the Joneses**
on the house	**live it up**
beneath one	**top-of-the-line**
right at one's feet	**have a blast**
take one's breath away	**take it easy**
make one's day	

9:04   What attractions does Mountaincrest have for tourists?

*Skiing, boating, horseback riding, and hiking, as well as many museums, art galleries, and cultural events—all of these activities are **easily accessible and available** to all visitors.*

There are a number of attractions right at your feet, such as skiing, boating, horseback riding, hiking, and a variety of museums, art galleries, and cultural events.

9:36   We're sick of eating at fast-food restaurants. Can you recommend a really good place to eat?

*One of the best restaurants in town, that serves the **highest quality** food, is called "The King's Feast."*

_____

10:15   My husband is very nervous because there have been several predictions of an earthquake in this region. Is there anything I can tell him so he won't worry so much?

*Tell him to **relax!** There have been no earthquakes in this area for more than 300 years!*

_____

10:20   We're looking for some beautiful scenery that we can take pictures of. Where should we go?

*There is a waterfall nearby that is so beautiful it will **astound you!***

_____

11:30   What activity would you recommend for small children?

*You should take them to the zoo—it's very small, but they'll **have a great time!***

_____

11:51   I don't have a question; I just wanted to tell you that I think you're doing a great job, and Mountaincrest is a wonderful town!

*Thank you! That **makes me very happy!***

12:12   I'm looking for a gift for a very special friend. Where should I shop?

*There are quite a few stores downtown that have unusual items that might **stand out.***

2:10   We're going to the theater tonight. How should we dress?

*We usually consider a play to be a very formal event, so **wear your finest clothing.***

2:37   My wife wanted to go to Atlantic City because our neighbors often go there on vacation. I finally convinced her to come to Mountaincrest, but she's not sure the neighbors will be impressed. What can I do to help her enjoy our vacation more?

*Tell her to quit worrying about **competing with your neighbors!** Besides, Mountaincrest was rated much higher than Atlantic City in **Tour Magazine.***

2:42   We spent the day up in the mountains, and now we're ready to do something in town. Is there anything going on tonight?

*There are various restaurants, clubs, bars, and dance halls open all night long. Why don't you **go out and enjoy yourselves!***

2:59   This year my wife and I are celebrating our thirtieth wedding anniversary, and we'd like to do something really special. Do you have any ideas?

*Reserve a suite at our finest hotel, eat at the best restaurants, and **enjoy yourselves to the fullest**—you will have a wonderful time no matter what you choose!*

3:48   We're touring with a very important businessman who is used to staying in the best suites of the finest hotels. Where should we stay?

*Your best option is the Mountaincrest Lodge—it is an excellent hotel, and any other accommodations would probably be considered **inferior to his usual standards.***

4:10   How much does it cost to stay at the Mountaincrest Lodge?

*It usually costs $200.00 a night, but all this month, if you stay there three nights, the fourth night is **free!***

II Finding the Idioms in Ads

INTERPRETING THE ADS

Look at the following advertisements. First determine what is being advertised and what idiom is featured in the ad. Review the meaning of the idiom. Then answer the questions corresponding to each ad.

1. What is the advantage of staying at ClubHouse Inns?

2. What do they offer free of charge?

1. How does the picture relate to the phrase "Mrs. Blume's science class is a blast"?

2. Is the phrase "a blast" used literally or idiomatically? Explain.

1. Describe the picture. What is happening? Who are the people in the picture? What are they doing?

2. What kind of lifestyle do you associate with "living it up"?

3. What point does this ad make?

1. How would the advertisers suggest that you "pass" the Joneses?

2. What is the message of this ad?

1. In what way is "the world's leading technology at your feet"?

2. How does the idiom relate to the product being advertised?

If it doesn't make your day, we'll make it over.

We'll make it hot. We'll make it fast. We'll make it just the way it should be. And if ever we don't, we'll make it right. Or your next meal's on us. It's the new McDonald's Guarantee. And it's here to stay. Hot food. Fast, friendly service. Drive-thru orders double-checked right. Our new way to make your day. What you want is what you get. GUARANTEED

Guarantee details at participating McDonald's. ©1992 McDonald's Corporation.

1. How does McDonald's want their customers to feel after they eat an order from their restaurant?

2. Another idiom, "make it right," is used in the text of the ad. What does it mean? How does this idiom relate to the first one?

THINKING ABOUT THE ADS

Review the ads from this chapter. Based on the messages contained in the ads, choose the one that you think best illustrates American cultural values. Complete statements one through four based on that ad.

1. This ad would appeal to an American audience because . . . .

2. It is important to many Americans to . . . .

3. Other examples in American life that show how Americans feel about this issue or value are . . . .

4. This ad would/would not appeal to an audience from my country because . . . .

5. The ad that I liked best is . . . .

6. The ad that made the best use of an idiom is . . . because . . . .

III Using the Idioms

USING THE IDIOMS IN SPEECH

A. One-minute Speech

Write a brief outline before presenting your one-minute speech to your classmates. Be sure to use the idioms from this chapter in your speech.

What is the best vacation you've ever had? Where did you go? What time of year did you go? Who went with you? What did you do there? How long did you stay? What was your favorite part of the vacation? Describe your vacation to your classmates.

B. Group Discussion

Participate in the following discussion, using the idioms from this chapter.

Many people believe that in order to be successful professionally or socially, they must look and act in a particular way rather than just "be themselves." Do you believe this is true? Discuss the following questions with your group: In order to impress and gain the acceptance of your business and social companions, is it necessary to

- dress in the latest styles?
- host occasional parties?
- spend evenings out on the town with your colleagues and associates?
- drive the "right" car, belong to the "right" clubs, or go to the "right" social events?

or is it better to just relax and not worry about what others think of you?

C. Debate: Retirement Options

Read the situation and choose to defend either side of the following question: Should Martha live in the retirement community or stay with her family? Before you begin, jot down the arguments supporting your position. Remember to use as many of the idioms from this chapter as you can.

Martha Dawson had been married for forty-eight years when her husband died, leaving her alone with no family members living close by. She doesn't want to spend the rest of her life living by herself, but she can't decide where she should go. She can choose to move to a retirement community where many of her friends live and where she could associate with people her age and with similar interests. There she would have her own comfortable apartment, and she could maintain a certain level of independence, but she could take her meals and participate in fun social activities in the main building. She could go on tours and outings with other residents of the community and spend her later years relaxing and having fun. However, Martha's son and his family have been begging her to come live with them, and they have even converted their garage into a small living space for her. Although they have four small children, her son insists that it would be no extra trouble providing for her as well. Martha would like to be near her family (the retirement community would be very far away), but she isn't sure she could take having so many kids around all the time, and she is worried that she would quickly lose her independence.

D. Role Plays

Imagine yourself in one of the situations described below. Act it out with another member of your class, using as many idioms from this chapter as you can in your conversation. You and your partner may want to write a brief script of the role play before acting it out.

1. (two college students)

STUDENT A: It is the week before final exams and you are feeling the pressure to do well and get good grades in all your classes. This is especially important to your parents, as they are quite anxious for you to do at least as well as their neighbor's daughter, who is at the same university. Even though you have been studying hard all year, you feel you must spend this last week studying harder than ever. When the exams are over, you will relax.

STUDENT B: Your friend is too uptight! He/She has received the top scores in every class and you're sure your friend's marks on the final exams will be just as good. You aren't quite so dedicated to your studies; why should you waste all your time in college studying when you could be out making friends and having fun? Try to convince your friend to come with you to a party at another student's apartment. A lot of great people will be there, and you know everyone will have a good time.

2. (the manager at the Laguna de Oro resort, a guest at the resort)

MANAGER: You are interested in knowing how your guests enjoyed their stay at the resort. Before they check out of the hotel, you usually ask them if the service was satisfactory. You also ask what special activities they engaged in and what they liked the best about their stay. To show your appreciation for their patronage, you sometimes offer a free meal at the restaurant in the hotel. Talk to this guest.

GUEST: You were generally pleased with your experience at the Laguna de Oro, although the friends you stayed with thought the accommodations were below their usual standards—they are used to rooms that are even more luxurious. However, you had a wonderful time sailing and relaxing in the courtyard. Tell the manager how much you liked the resort.

USING THE IDIOMS IN WRITING

E. Writing with Idioms

Read the unfinished story below. What happens next? Imagine how the story ends, and write an appropriate conclusion, using the idioms from this chapter.

The phone was ringing on two different lines, a group of clients were standing in the hallway arguing, the secretaries' typewriters tapped on incessantly, and the fax machine was beeping again. Richard's head was spinning; he simply couldn't take it anymore. The noise and confusion were too much for him. He put his head down on his desk for a moment and groaned wearily. "What I need is a genie to take me away from all of this," he thought to himself. Suddenly he noticed that the sounds all around him began to dim. The phones stopped ringing. There were no beeping noises, no angry voices, not even any sirens or honking from the traffic outside his window. Richard held his breath and very slowly lifted his head. It was quiet! And in the armchair facing his desk there was a tiny wrinkled woman. "I am your genie," she said in a squeaky voice, "but I'm very busy, and I can only give you one day, so you must use it well. Where would you like to go?"

"Ah," Richard sighed, as a brilliant smile spread across his face, "I know just the place."

F. Advertising with Idioms

Make up an advertisement for any type of product not *advertised in the ads in this chapter, using one or more of the idioms you have just learned. Follow the steps listed below.*

1. Choose a product or service that you would like to advertise.

2. Determine your audience—the people most likely to buy your product or service.

3. Determine what value(s) would appeal to that audience. How are you going to incorporate that value into your ad?

4. Make up a slogan, using one of the idioms from this chapter.

5. Decide what visual cues (pictures, etc.) will accompany the slogan.

6. Write the rest of the ad.

7. Present it to the class. Do you think this ad would appeal to the other members of your class?

ARGUING

Idioms

MAKE MOUNTAINS OUT OF MOLEHILLS

GET A RISE OUT OF SOMEONE

DRIVE SOMEONE CRAZY

CHEAP SHOT

SHOW ONE'S TRUE COLORS

MEAN BEANS

TAKE A HIKE

FOUR-LETTER WORDS

COULDN'T CARE LESS

CUT IT OUT

GIVE SOMEONE A BREAK

CLEAR THE AIR

I Learning the Idioms

WARMING UP

Complete the following activity in small groups of three to five students. Compare answers and discuss with your classmates.

1. What was the subject of the last major disagreement you had with someone? How was it resolved?

2. What would make you most angry? Rank the following scenarios from 1 (most angry) to 8 (least angry). Discuss the kinds of situations that make you and your classmates angry.

    ——— a. Your neighbor always plays loud music late at night when you are trying to sleep.

    ——— b. You overhear a conversation between two people you know— they are talking about you, and it isn't very complimentary!

    ——— c. You have a very important appointment, and the person who was supposed to pick you up is an hour late.

    ——— d. Your teacher accuses you of cheating on a test, but it's not true!

    ——— e. A waiter in a restaurant spills soup all over your new clothes.

    ——— f. You discover your roommate has been stealing money from you.

    ——— g. When you first arrive in the United States, an airline official informs you that all your luggage is on its way to Indonesia; it was accidentally put on the wrong airplane.

    ——— h. Your girl/boyfriend is cheating on you (going out with another man/woman).

3. Think of three phrases in your native tongue that you might use if you were angry or arguing with someone. What do they mean?

4. How do you react to confrontations? From the following list, check off the reaction you would be most likely to have if you disagreed with someone. What are the advantages and disadvantages of each type of reaction?

    ———a. You argue your point strongly.

    ———b. You give in immediately and admit you were wrong.

    ———c. You try to discuss the matter calmly and reach a mutual understanding.

    ———d. You feel very uncomfortable; you generally try to avoid all confrontations.

GETTING TO KNOW THE IDIOMS

A. Listening for Understanding

Listen to the following conversation between a man and women.
Consider these questions as you listen to their conversation.
Afterward, discuss the answers with your classmates in pairs or
small groups.

1. What was the relationship between Sara and Danny before their confrontation? And after?

2. Why was Sara angry?

3. What was Danny's explanation of what happened? Do you believe it?

4. With whom do you sympathize more—Sara or Danny? Why?

5. If you were in Sara's situation, how would you handle it? How about if you were in Danny's place?

6. What do you think is going to happen next (with Danny, his secretary, Sara, and Mr. Galvin)?

B. Identifying the Idioms

Next, read the dialogue to which you have just listened.
Throughout the conversation you will find the idioms listed below.
Underline the idioms, and number them on the list in the order in
which you find them. Can you tell what they mean by how they are
used?

_____ **cheap shot**

_____ **make mountains out of molehills**

_____ **clear the air**

_____ **mean beans**

_____ **take a hike**

_____ **four-letter words**

_____ **show one's true colors**

_____ **give someone a break**

_____ **couldn't care less**

_____ **get a rise out of someone**

_____ **cut it out**

_____ **drive someone crazy**

MAKING MOUNTAINS OUT OF MOLEHILLS

DANNY: Sara, please don't leave. I think we just need to clear the air. If you will give me a chance to explain, I'm sure you will see that you're making mountains out of molehills. Nothing happened! There is no reason for you to be upset!

SARA: Oh, yeah? Nothing happened? No reason to be upset? So, is kissing your secretary after work a common occurrence? I saw it all; you don't have to explain anything. It was all quite clear!

DANNY: Sara, I swear she doesn't mean beans to me! It wasn't what it looked like. Honestly, I couldn't care less about her. You are the only one for me, and I couldn't bear to lose you. Please wait!

SARA: Well, now you are showing your true colors. You are obviously a liar as well as a cheat. And all this time I thought you were an honorable man. It's a good thing I found out what you are really like before it was too late. You can't possibly expect me to believe your story after watching your passionate embrace with your secretary. Take a hike!

DANNY: Give me a break, Sara. I told you I can explain everything. Just listen to me for a minute, and you'll understand. Remember, I listened to you after I found your old boyfriend sleeping in your apartment.

SARA: Now that was a cheap shot, Danny. You know that was different! He was in the garage, not my apartment, and I certainly wasn't kissing him! I saw you kissing your secretary; you can't deny it. I can't believe I ever trusted you. You're just a . . . a . . .

DANNY: Cut it out. Four-letter words aren't going to help you. Just listen to me! You see, my secretary's old boyfriend, Mr. Galvin, from the other office, broke up with her a couple of months ago. She was devastated. She spent half the day crying, and she wasn't getting any work done. She was driving me crazy! Finally, I suggested that she do something to try to get him back. She thought she could get a rise out of him if he saw her with another man. She said it would make him jealous. So I agreed to help her out. I guess it didn't work.

SARA: Mr. Galvin? You mean Chip Galvin, that handsome man that invited me out for a cup of coffee last week? Well, it's no wonder she was in love with him! He's such a charming man—and *so* handsome! Oh, here he comes now! I think I'll accept that invitation!

C. Getting the Meaning

Notice the highlighted phrase in each of the following sentences. Pay attention to how the idiom is used, and try to guess its meaning. You may also refer to the preceding dialogue. Write the meaning of the idiom on the line. The first one is done for you.

1. Sam and Nicole have been arguing a lot lately. I think they need to **clear the air**.

   get rid of the bad feelings between them
   _____

2. Mrs. Greenbaum threatened to complain to the manager because I overcharged her by three cents. She's always **making mountains out of molehills**.

   _____

3. "Stephanie, I'm sorry about last night. Can't we talk about it?"
   "No! I don't want to talk to you right now. **Take a hike!**"

   _____

4. The grade you got in your last English class doesn't **mean beans** to me. I'm only interested in the work you do in my class.

   _____

5. He thought he could impress me by telling me about all the movie stars he knows; in truth, I **couldn't care less**.

_____

6. Mr. Grady seemed to be a perfect gentleman until he lost the election. He **showed his true colors** when he began angrily accusing his opponent of cheating and his own campaign workers of being traitors.

_____

7. You know, I think John feels really bad about what happened. Why don't you **give him a break** and talk to him?

_____

8. When they were fighting for custody of their child, Mrs. Selway brought up the time little Jimmy broke his arm while he was in her ex-husband's care. That was a **cheap shot**; she knows that wasn't his fault!

_____

9. I can't work with all the noise you're making! **Cut it out** right now!

_____

10. I went to a movie yesterday that was rated for family viewing and I was shocked at the language! Why do they have to use so many **four-letter words?**

_____

11. Would you please turn down the radio? That music is **driving me crazy**!

_____

12. Christopher put a fake spider on Melissa's seat this morning to see if he could **get a rise out of her**.

_____

PRACTICING THE IDIOMS

D. Choosing the Best Answer

Listen carefully to the following taped statements. Read the choices listed below for each statement you hear. Select the sentence that best relates to the original statement, and circle the corresponding letter.

1. a. What a cheap shot!
   b. You gave me a break!
   c. You cleared the air!

2. a. He should take a hike.
   b. We ought to clear the air.
   c. He showed his true colors.

3. a. You couldn't care less.
   b. It was a cheap shot.
   c. You're making mountains out of molehills.

4. a. Let's clear the air!
   b. Give me a break!
   c. Cut it out!

5. a. We need to clear the air.
   b. I couldn't care less.
   c. Use some four-letter words.

6. a. He made mountains out of molehills.
   b. He couldn't care less.
   c. He got a rise out of her.

7. a. It doesn't mean beans to me.
   b. It's a cheap shot.
   c. It clears the air.

8. a. He just wanted to get a rise out of her.
   b. He wanted to give her a break.
   c. He wanted her to take a hike.

9. a. Show your true colors!
   b. Give me a break!
   c. Take a hike!

10. a. I wish I could get a rise out of him.
    b. I wish he would cut it out.
    c. It doesn't mean beans to me.

11. a. You should make mountains out of molehills.
     b. You should take a hike.
     c. You should never use four-letter words.

12. a. She drives me crazy.
     b. She means beans to me.
     c. She gives me a break.

E. Retelling the Story—Optional Activity

*Read the dialogue on pages 150–151 again. The sentences below
refer to statements in that dialogue. On the lines below, restate the
sentences, using the appropriate idiom in each one. The first one is
done for you.*

1. Danny wanted to get rid of the angry feelings between him and Sara.

    Danny wanted to clear the air.

2. He thought Sara was exaggerating the importance of the incident.

3. Danny claimed that his secretary didn't mean anything to him.

4. He said that he didn't care at all for her.

5. Sara said that Danny was revealing what he was really like.

6. She told him to go away.

7. Danny begged her to give him a chance.

8. When Danny brought up Sara's old boyfriend, she said it was an unfair
    comparison.

9. Danny told her to stop it.

10. He said that swearing at him wouldn't help the situation.

_____

11. He claimed that his secretary had been annoying him greatly because she was so lovesick for her ex-boyfriend.

_____

12. Danny's secretary thought she could get a strong reaction from Mr. Galvin if he saw her with another man.

_____

F. Putting the Idioms into Practice

You are a well-known advice columnist for a big newspaper. Each week you receive hundreds of letters about problems people have. Your assistant reads the letters and chooses the most interesting problems. Then she briefly summarizes their main points and gives you a report. As you read the report from your assistant, write your immediate impressions beneath each problem, choosing from the statements below.

Money means beans to him!

She's driving him crazy!

That's a cheap shot!

It's time to clear the air!

Tell him to take a hike!

He's showing his true colors!

Four-letter words are inappropriate!

He obviously couldn't care less!

She's making mountains out of molehills!

Tell them to cut it out!

Give him a break!

He wants to get a rise out of them!

1. A citizen is angry because a politician she supported has not fulfilled his campaign promises. He promised to get tougher laws for criminals, but now he's letting a lot of them out of prison *early*.

   _____

2. A woman writes that a prospective employer told her that he would not hire her simply because he thinks she is ugly, and could not project the desired image for the company.

   _____

3. A man claims that his wife is threatening to divorce him because he squeezes the tube of toothpaste wrong.

   _____

4. A man told his employer that he was sick when, in fact, he spent the day at the beach with his friends. The boss found out and fired him, but now the former employee is begging for another chance. The man's boss doesn't know what to do.

   _____

5. Several years ago two sisters fell in love with the same man. Although the man long ago married someone else, the two sisters haven't spoken to each other for years. Now one of the women wants to reconcile the bad feelings between them.

   _____

6. A woman has spent her whole life trying to please her father, but he never seems to notice or be impressed by any of her accomplishments.

   _____

7. A man's wife has always pushed him to work harder and longer hours so they can have more money, but he wants to slow down and take it easy. He doesn't care how much he makes; he just wants to enjoy life a little more.

   _____

8. A man working in an office with several women likes to tell off-color jokes to his female co-workers. The women are offended and don't know how to handle the situation.

   _____

9. A man has cheated on his girlfriend with more than ten different women, and every time it happens, he cries and tells her he's sorry and that it will never happen again. She has always taken him back, but she knows he will probably take advantage of her again.

_____

10. A woman reports that after every party at her neighbors' house, she finds a mess in her own backyard. Her neighbors dump all of the trash from their parties over the fence for her to clean up.

_____

11. A teenager has frequent arguments with her father. Although her father doesn't physically abuse her, his language is crude and offensive. He swears at her and calls her bad names. She feels very depressed over this.

_____

12. A man's girlfriend is very indecisive, and he is becoming increasingly irritated. For example, she will say she wants Chinese food, but when they get to the restaurant, she decides Mexican food would be better. She wants to go to a movie, and then halfway through it, she'll say she would rather go dancing. Her boyfriend just can't take it anymore.

_____

II Finding the Idioms in Ads

INTERPRETING THE ADS

Look at the following advertisements. First determine what is being advertised and what idiom is featured in the ad. Review the meaning of the idiom. Then answer the questions corresponding to each ad.

5:48 p.m. Trekking through the Southern Alps, New Zealand.

[For a free color catalog including full details of our lifetime warranty and the location of your nearest North Face dealer call 1-800-654-1751.]

Your RENT is LATE, your GOLDFISH is probably DEAD and you think you've LEFT the IRON ON. YOU couldn't CARE LESS.

You're checking out a view that makes an Ansel Adams print look like a snapshot from one of those disposable cameras. But maybe the best part is you're 8,000 miles from the nearest Winnebago. For over twenty years, outdoor gear from The North Face has been helping people go places where people weren't supposed to go. Like scaling the 5.14a "Scarface" route at Smith Rock, Oregon. Or circling the base of Everest on skis. Which may be why The North Face has been the choice of practically every major expedition of the past two decades. And like them, you can expect every article of clothing, every tent, pack and sleeping bag we make to be guaranteed for life. Because, for us, it has always come down to one thing: making clothing and equipment whose performance you can take for granted. So you can concentrate on why you're out there in the first place.

THE NORTH FACE

1. What is it, according to this ad, that you "couldn't care less" about? Why?

2. What do the advertisers think you should care about?

1. What is happening in the picture?

2. Why is the driver "driving himself crazy"?

3. What would the advertisers suggest doing to solve the problem?

1. Why do the advertisers want us to "give eggs a break"? What does that mean?

2. Is the phrase used literally, idiomatically, or both? Explain.

3. Why do you think the egg is shown in jail? (Another idiom with the word break is to break out of, meaning to escape from.)

1. Describe the man in the picture. How does one arm differ from the other?

2. In this ad, what do "mountains" and "molehills" refer to?

3. What is the purpose of AMF products?

4. Why do you think the advertisers used this idiom to gain attention for their products?

1. In this ad, does "four-letter words" refer to bad or vulgar words? What does it refer to?

2. Is the statement "It's amazing how quickly kids start using four-letter words" meant in a literal, an idiomatic sense, or both? Explain.

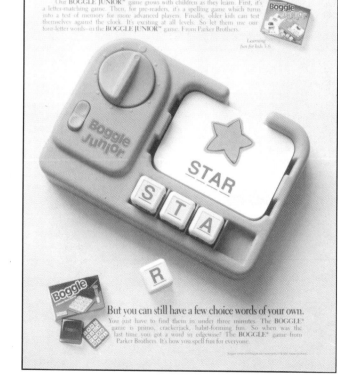

1. Look at the picture. With what is the basket filled? (Jelly beans are a popular candy in the United States, and are often given to children at Eastertime).

2. Is the idiom in this ad used literally, idiomatically, or both? Explain.

Does Easter mean beans to your kids?

If you agree that Easter should do more for your children than raise their blood sugar level, we invite you and your family to experience the true miracle of Easter in The Episcopal Church.
The Episcopal Church

THINKING ABOUT THE ADS

Review the ads from this chapter. Based on the messages contained in the ads, choose the one that you think best illustrates American cultural values. Complete statements one through four based on that ad.

1. This ad would appeal to an American audience because . . . .

2. It is important to many Americans to . . . .

3. Other examples in American life that show how Americans feel about this issue or value are . . . .

4. This ad would/would not appeal to an audience from my country because . . . .

5. The ad that I liked the best is . . . .

6. The ad that made the best use of an idiom is . . . because . . . .

III Using the Idioms

USING THE IDIOMS IN SPEECH

A. One-minute Speech

Write a brief outline before presenting your one-minute speech to your classmates. Be sure to use the idioms from this chapter in your speech.

Can you remember the last major argument you had with someone? What was the nature of the disagreement? Were both parties angry, or just one person? Why? Tell the members of your group what happened during this encounter (or any other argument you are willing to describe, whether or not you were directly involved).

B. Group Discussion

Participate in the following discussion, using the idioms from this chapter.

There are many common proverbs that deal with both the positive and negative aspects of relationships. Several of these proverbs are listed below. First, try to figure out what each of the proverbs means. Then, choose three and discuss them, giving examples to illustrate their meanings. Are there similar expressions in your language? Discuss those as well.

- Misery loves company.
- Familiarity breeds contempt.
- Don't bite the hand that feeds you.
- Don't burn your bridges behind you.
- Don't cut off your nose to spite your face.
- Fight fire with fire.
- People in glass houses shouldn't throw stones.
- You can attract more bees with honey than you can with vinegar.

C. Debate: Generalizations

As you read each of the controversial statements listed below, decide whether you agree or disagree. Debate the issue for a few minutes with your partner, who will defend the opposite viewpoint, and then quickly move on to the next statement. Be sure to use as many of the idioms from this chapter as you can.

- Women are smarter than men.

- People who live in large cities are rude.

- Life in the United States is easy.

- American food is terrible.

- Cigarette smoking should be banned from all public places.

- TV and movie violence creates a more aggressive and violent society.

- Censorship is sometimes necessary.

D. Role Plays

Imagine yourself in one of the situations described below. Act it out with another member of your class, using as many idioms from this chapter as you can in your conversation. You and your partner may want to write a brief script for the role play before acting it out.

1. (two siblings)

SIBLING A: Two nights ago you started watching a terrific show on television. It is being broadcast in three parts, and tonight is the exciting conclusion. You have rearranged your schedule so that you can see what happens tonight and how the show ends. There is only one TV in your home.

SIBLING B: Your English teacher told you that if you would watch a special educational program that is on television tonight and write a short report on it, he would give you some extra points in the class. You haven't been doing very well in the class, and you know you have to improve your grade. This is a perfect opportunity, and you need to take advantage of it! Talk to your brother/sister about it.

2. (Danny, Sara)

DANNY: You feel very bad about what happened at the office yesterday. Sara left with Mr. Galvin, and your secretary is just as upset as you are. Call Sara and try to convince her to give you another chance.

SARA: You feel great about the ways things turned out. After spending several hours with Chip Galvin yesterday, you realized that Danny was the wrong person for you all along. You are looking forward to spending more time with Chip, whom you like and respect much more. When Danny calls, tell him that your relationship is over.

USING THE IDIOMS IN WRITING

E. Writing with Idioms

Write a news report based on the situation described below, using the idioms from this chapter.

The media, especially tabloid newspapers, often make much of celebrity couples when they get together as well as when they split apart. Imagine you are a reporter for one of these tabloids and you have been assigned to write a sensational story about the breakup of a famous couple. Describe their relationship, and report on the dramatic arguments they had in public. Tell what (or who) caused the breakup.

F. Advertising with Idioms

Make up an advertisement for any type of product not advertised in the ads in this chapter, using one or more of the idioms you have just learned. Follow the steps listed below.

1. Choose a product or service that you would like to advertise.

2. Determine your audience—the people most likely to buy your product or service.

3. Determine what value(s) would appeal to that audience. How are you going to incorporate that value into your ad?

4. Make up a slogan, using one of the idioms from this chapter.

5. Decide what visual cues (pictures, etc.) will accompany the slogan.

6. Write the rest of the ad.

7. Present it to the class. Do you think this ad would appeal to the other members of your class?

Idioms

DOESN'T GROW ON TREES

IN THE RED

IN THE BLACK

STRETCHED TOO THIN

COST (OR CHARGE) AN ARM AND A LEG

TAKE SOMEONE TO THE CLEANERS

FOR A SONG

BOUNCE A CHECK

COUGH UP

HANG ON

LIVE WITHIN ONE'S MEANS

SEARCH HIGH AND LOW

GET ONE'S HANDS ON SOMETHING

STAY PUT

Living well within your means.

soft, soft touch of cotton made carefree with Fortrel®
blossoms on 180 thread count ready to be plucked from
Cannon. For stores nearest you call 1-800-237-3209.

the Living Legacies.
Or write Cannon Mills, 1271 Avenue of the Americas, New York, NY 10020.

FORTREL
The Fiber of Choice   Fortrel is a trademark of Fiber Industries, Inc. for premium polyester

CANNON
THE FABRIC OF LIFE

Coordinate with Cannon for lively sales.

The smartly priced, coordinated beauty of Cannon's Living Legacy Collection will really hit home with the 30 million plus readers who'll see this ad in leading magazines like Home, Country Living and Better Homes & Gardens.

So be sure to stock up on the entire line. And find out how lively sales can be when you coordinate with Cannon.

CANNON
THE FABRIC OF LIFE

I Learning the Idioms

WARMING UP

Complete the following activity in small groups of three to five students. Compare answers and discuss with your classmates.

1. With the other members of your group, figure out a reasonable monthly budget for living in the city you are in. Decide on the average amount of money people spend on the following items per month. What is the total amount? Compare your figures with those of other groups.

Rent	$ _____
Food	$ _____
Transportation	$ _____
Medical Care	$ _____
Education	$ _____
Entertainment	$ _____
Clothing	$ _____
Utilities (gas, electricity, etc.)	$ _____
Telephone	$ _____
Other? _____	$ _____
TOTAL	$ _____

What is the least amount of money you think you would need each month to survive in this city? How does that figure compare to the cost of living in your native country?

2. Which of the following items do you own? Which do you consider necessities? Which do you consider luxuries?

refrigerator	tapes or CDs	scissors
car	sports equipment	games (cards, etc.)
stereo	computer	watch
television	radio	telephone
books	stove	bicycle

3. If you were given $50, how would you spend it? $500? $5,000? $50,000? $1,000,000? Compare answers with those of your classmates.

GETTING TO KNOW THE IDIOMS

A. Listening for Understanding

Listen to a series of letters from a young man to his father. Consider these questions as you listen to the letters. Afterward, discuss the answers with your classmates in pairs or small groups.

1. Where do you think Harry is? Where do you think he came from?

2. What are three challenges Harry has faced since coming to the city? Have you ever been in a similar situation?

3. How did Joe help Harry? What did Joe warn him about?

4. Have you ever lived on your own? What was the most difficult adjustment you had to make?

5. Do you think life in a big city is easier or harder than in a small town? Why? How is it different? Which do you prefer? Why?

B. Identifying the Idioms

Next, read the letters to which you have just listened. Throughout these letters you will find the idioms listed below. Underline the idioms, and number them on the list in the order in which you find them. Can you tell what they mean by how they are used?

_____ get one's hands on something   _____ doesn't grow on trees

_____ bounce a check   _____ hang on

_____ for a song   _____ live within one's means

_____ search high and low   _____ cough up

_____ cost an arm and a leg   _____ stretched too thin

_____ in the red   _____ take someone to the cleaners

_____ in the black   _____ stay put

LIVING WITHIN YOUR MEANS

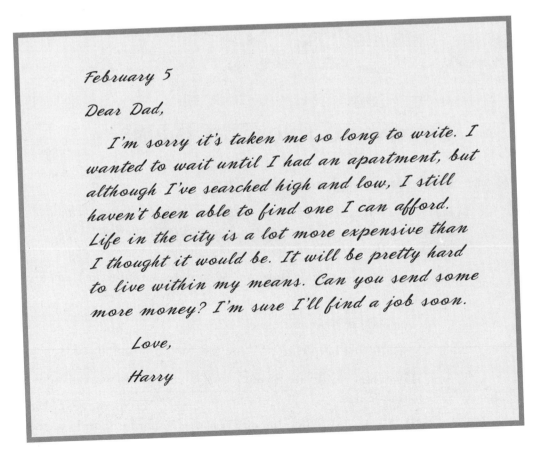

February 5

Dear Dad,

I'm sorry it's taken me so long to write. I wanted to wait until I had an apartment, but although I've searched high and low, I still haven't been able to find one I can afford. Life in the city is a lot more expensive than I thought it would be. It will be pretty hard to live within my means. Can you send some more money? I'm sure I'll find a job soon.

Love,

Harry

February 27
Dear Dad,

I know you're doing the best you can, but I can't live on $50 a week! Everything here costs an arm and a leg, so I would really appreciate it if you could send a little more. I tried to get my hands on a used car so it would be easier to get out and look for a job, but I've had no luck. One man said he could get me a good deal on an old Chevy, but he wanted me to cough up $500 <u>before</u> I even saw the car! Meanwhile, my bank account keeps getting smaller. I've already bounced one check, so now the corner supermarket will only accept cash from me. I am just stretched too thin. Can't you help me please?

Love,
Harry

March 19
Dear Dad,

Thanks for the cash. I'll try to hang on until I get a job. I had an interview a couple of days ago, and I thought it went really well, but they decided to hire someone else instead. I'm getting kind of desperate—you know money doesn't grow on trees, and I've got bills to pay! Do you think you could send a little more? I'll let you know as soon as I find a job.

Love,
Harry

April 2

Dear Dad,

I love this city! I'm finally ready to settle down and stay put. Last week, I met a guy whose sister I knew in high school, and he has really helped me a lot. His name is Joe Forrester. He warned me that a man who was going to rent me an apartment would try to take me to the cleaners, so Joe offered to let me stay in the basement of his house. It's a cozy little place on the west side of town, and because I don't have much money, he's letting me have it for a song! Joe also talked to his boss about finding me a job, and guess what! I start work on Monday! Finally my bank account will be in the black again—I am getting tired of always being in the red. I knew everything would work out in the end. Thanks for your help. I'll call you soon.

Love,

Harry

C. Getting the Meaning

Notice the highlighted phrase in each of the following sentences. Pay attention to how the idiom is used, and try to guess its meaning. You may also refer to the preceding letters. Write the meaning of the idiom on the line. The first one is done for you.

1. Molly **searched high and low** for shoes that would match her new dress, but she couldn't find the right color.

   to look everywhere for something
   _____

2. Mr. Jensen is a janitor, and his wife stays home to take care of their five children. I don't know how they can **live within their means**.

   _____

3. Don't buy anything in the stores on Rodeo Drive. They'll charge **an arm and a leg** for everything.

   _____

4. A new music store in Hollywood was giving away tickets to the Janet Jackson concert. I tried to **get my hands on a couple of them**, but they were all gone by the time I had reached the front of the line.

_____

5. Mrs. Simpson, I know you lost your job, but this apartment isn't free. You are going to have to **cough up** the rent soon, or else leave. I'm sorry.

_____

6. I wrote a check for $246, but there was only $211 in my account. If I **bounce a check** again, the bank is going to cancel my account.

_____

7. I'll have to borrow some money to pay my bills this month. With my wife's surgery, car repairs, and our son's college tuition, I'm **stretched too thin**.

_____

8. The economy is very weak in some parts of the country, but if the people can **hang on**, I'm sure the situation will eventually improve.

_____

9. Marie, I would love to buy you a new dress for the prom, but it's too expensive. You know that **money doesn't grow on trees**.

_____

10. Sheila has moved to a different city almost every year since she left home. However, this time she says she likes it enough to **stay put** for a while.

_____

11. The art dealer told me it was an original Renoir and that the value of the painting had tripled over the last year. I'm glad I didn't buy it—he would have really **taken me to the cleaners**.

_____

12. The man that sold me my car was so nice! He knew I was a student and couldn't afford very much, so he gave it to me **for a song**.

_____

13. General Motors has been losing money for many years, but with the economy improving, they are finally operating **in the black** again.

_____

14. Jenny doesn't know how to manage her money. The bank has to call periodically to tell her she's **in the red** again.

_____

PRACTICING THE IDIOMS

D. Choosing the Best Answer

Listen carefully to the following statements. Decide if the sentence that corresponds to each is true or false. Circle T if it is true and F if it is false.

1. T / F I didn't spend much time shopping for her.

2. T / F Ellen manages her money carefully.

3. T / F I bought the sofa for much less than it had cost at a different store.

4. T / F Gordon put his fingerprints on a very valuable piece of art.

5. T / F I couldn't spend the rent money on anything else.

6. T / F The bank won't know how much money you have in your account.

7. T / F Jeffrey is already involved in several different activities.

8. T / F Although it's difficult, Melissa continues to make an effort in her class.

9. T / F Sara and the men she has dated live in an area where there aren't many trees.

10. T / F Mr. Burr has moved around a lot in the past.

11. T / F They cleaned my car after repairing it.

12. T / F It's cheaper to buy a ticket if you can sing well.

13. T / F This company has made a profit for several months now.

14. T / F I have no further debts to pay off.

E. Retelling the Story—Optional Activity

Read the letters on pages 168–170 again. The sentences below refer to statements in those letters. On the lines below, restate the sentences, using the appropriate idiom in each one. The first one is done for you.

1. Harry looked everywhere for an apartment, but couldn't find one.

   Harry searched high and low for an apartment, but he wasn't able to find one.

2. He thinks it will be difficult to only spend the amount of money he had previously budgeted to live in the city.

   _____

3. Everything is extremely expensive.

   _____

4. Harry tried to get a car but wasn't able to.

   _____

5. The man who tried to sell him a car said that Harry had to come up with $500 before he could even see it!

   _____

6. Harry wrote a check for which he didn't have enough money in his account.

   _____

7. He has too many expenses and not enough money to cover them.

   _____

8. Harry says he will try to endure his situation until he can get a job.

   _____

9. Everyone knows that money is not readily available.

   _____

10. Harry is finally ready to stop moving around from place to place.

    _____

11. A man was trying to overcharge Harry for an apartment.

    _____

12. Joe is letting Harry stay in his basement for very little money.

    _____

13. When he starts working, Harry will finally be out of debt.

    _____

14. Harry is tired of having so much debt.

    _____

F. Putting the Idioms into Practice

In a widely read business newspaper, a regular columnist named "Manny" answers readers' questions about financial issues and gives them advice on how to spend their money. Read the following letters. Substitute one of the idioms listed below for each of the numbered phrases. Change the idioms as needed to fit the sentences.

search high and low	live within one's means	cost an arm and a leg
cough up	bounce a check	get one's hands on something
stretched too thin	hang on	doesn't grow on trees
stay put	for a song	take someone to the cleaners
in the red	in the black	

> *Dear Manny,*
>
> *For the last five years I've lived close enough to my job to have always walked to work. Now I am about to move, so I need a car. I am on a very limited budget. Can you give me some advice on getting a good deal on a car?*
>
> *Sincerely,*
>
> *Carla*

Dear Carla,

The first thing I would advise you to do is _____. Obviously, if you
                                          1. not to move

can avoid having to _____ the money for a car, you will be better off.
                    2. come up with

If you are _____ now, you will probably have a very difficult
          3. financially overextended

time _____ after you buy a car. Remember that besides
    4. living within your budget

the cost of the vehicle, gasoline, repairs, and insurance often _____.
                                                               5. cost a great deal

However, if you are determined, I would suggest buying a used car rather than a

new one. You might find someone willing to give you a previously owned car

_____.
6. for very little money

Dear Manny,

My favorite hobby is stamp collecting, and over the years, I have put together a fairly impressive collection. Recently, a man asked if I would be interested in buying a very rare stamp from the 1800s. It is a great opportunity to add to my collection, and besides, I'm sure it will continue to increase in value. The problem is that I would have to go into debt to buy it. What should I do?

Sincerely,

Walter

Dear Walter,

I can tell that you would love to —————————— this particular stamp for your
　　　　　　　　　　　　　　　　　　　7. acquire
collection, but I don't think it is worth it if you have to —————————— . I
　　　　　　　　　　　　　　　　　　　　　　　　　　　8. go into debt
recommend first of all that you have the stamp appraised so you can be certain of its

actual value. This man may be trying to —————————— .Then I
　　　　　　　　　　　　　　　　　9. cheat you and get more than the stamp's real worth
would —————————— for similar stamps; it may not be as rare as you
　　　10. conduct an extensive search
think. I know that truly valuable stamps —————————— , but perhaps if
　　　　　　　　　　　　　　　　　　　11. are not readily available
you can —————————— for a while longer, you will have another opportu-
　　　　12. persevere
nity to buy one when you have more money. Above all, don't try to buy it if you don't

have enough money in your checking account to cover it. It's against the law to inten-

tionally —————————— . Besides, it's just common sense to stay
　　　　　13. write a bad check
—————————— . You'll be much better off in the end.
　14. out of debt

II Finding the Idioms in Ads

INTERPRETING THE ADS

Look at the following advertisements. First determine what is being advertised and what idiom is featured in the ad. Review the meaning of the idiom. Then answer the questions corresponding to each ad.

1. Where do swings often hang?

2. What is the idiomatic meaning of "great swings don't grow on trees"? Is there another meaning?

Great swings don't grow on trees. They're made by Fisher-Price.

Fisher-Price® believes that a swing should be as friendly to parents as it is to kids. That's why we included special features in our Lift and Lock Swing.

Like a safety bar that lifts with one hand and stays up and out of the way until you're ready to lock your toddler securely in place.

And a high-backed contoured seat for extra comfort and support.

Durable, weather-resistant construction that won't rust or crack, with built-in drainage holes that keep yesterday's showers from spoiling today's smiles.

Fisher-Price Lift and Lock Swings don't actually grow on trees, but they do make them a lot more fun.

© 1991 Fisher-Price, East Aurora, New York 14052. Also available in Canada.

Safety bar stays up until you pull it down.

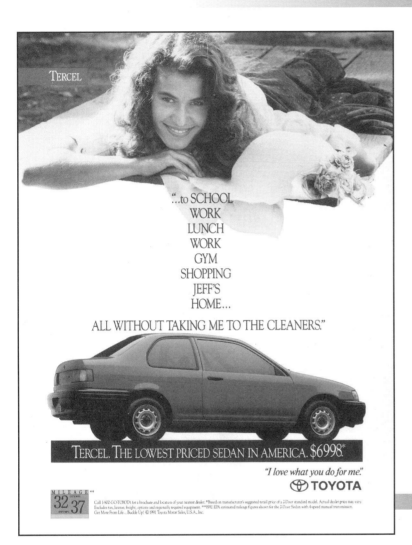

1. What does the list (to school, work, lunch, etc.) refer to?

2. Could "the cleaners" also have been on that list?

3. What is the underlying message of this ad?

1. What is "Luden's"?

2. Part of this ad is a coupon. What is a coupon? What does this one offer?

3. Why is this idiom especially appropriate for this ad?

1. There are two prominent idioms in this ad. Can you identify them? What do you think they mean?

2. How do those two expressions relate to one another?

1. Why did Cannon use this particular idiom? What do they want you to think about their product?

2. What does the picture indicate about the product?

THINKING ABOUT THE ADS

Review the ads from this chapter. Based on the messages contained in the ads, choose the one that you think best illustrates American cultural values. Complete statements one through four based on that ad.

1. This ad would appeal to an American audience because . . . .

2. It is important to many Americans to . . . .

3. Other examples in American life that show how Americans feel about this issue or value are . . . .

4. This ad would/would not appeal to an audience from my country because . . . .

5. The ad that I liked the best is . . . .

6. The ad that made the best use of an idiom is . . . because . . . .

III Using The Idioms

USING THE IDIOMS IN SPEECH

A. One-minute Speech

Write a brief outline before presenting your one-minute speech to your classmates. Be sure to use the idioms from this chapter in your speech.

Have you ever lived on your own, independent of anyone else's financial assistance? If you have, tell about your first experience of trying to make it on your own. Was it difficult to live within your means? Why? Tell your classmates about your experiences. If you have never lived on your own, tell how you think you would do it.

B. Group Discussion

Participate in the following discussion, using the idioms from this chapter.

You are all on the lending committee at a large bank. It is your job to determine to whom you should give a loan. The bank loses a lot of money on bad loans, so it is important to accurately determine the credit risk of the loan applicants. You have been authorized to give only one of the following people a loan for $15,000. Who will it be? What are the terms of your loan? Are there any conditions the applicants must meet? When must they begin repaying the loan? How much will their monthly payments be?

LEONA BATES—32 YEARS OLD

- Has two small children

- Never married; does not receive financial assistance from the children's father

- Dropped out of high school but later completed the necessary requirements to graduate; now attends a junior college

- Wants to be a school teacher; needs the money to complete her education

- Has worked for five years as a teacher's aide in an elementary school; has received very positive evaluations

JARED NORTH—51 YEARS OLD

- Has one adult son, still at home

- Worked for twenty-six years at a car factory; was fired last year because of chronic alcoholism

- Says he has stopped drinking

- Works for a delivery service now, but needs a new van if he is going to be able to keep his job; his old one keeps breaking down

ESTHER AND GEORGE BENSON—BOTH IN THEIR LATE 40S

- No children

- Met and married when they were both working for an interior design company

- Would like to start their own business

- The field of interior design is highly competitive, but they have an extensive list of clients that they say have agreed to follow them.

C. Debate: Parental Responsibility

Read the situation and choose to defend either side of the following question: Should Diana's parents take her in again? *Before you begin, jot down the arguments supporting your position. Remember to use as many of the idioms from this chapter as you can.*

Diana had never been very responsible with her money. She always spent more than she had and then relied on her parents to come to her rescue. She could never hold a job for longer than three months, and consequently, she never moved out of her parent's home. Finally, shortly after Diana turned twenty-eight years old, her parents had had enough. Although they loved her very much, they felt she needed to learn to be responsible for herself. They told her she could no longer live with them, and that they wouldn't pay her bills anymore. After they helped her find a job and an apartment, they said their parental responsibility to take care of her was over. Several months later, however, Diana was again jobless; and this time she was living on the streets, surrounded by crime and danger. She begged her parents to let her come home again. What should they do?

D. Role Plays

Imagine yourself in one of the situations described below. Act it out with another member of your class, using as many idioms from this chapter as you can in your conversation. You and your partner may want to write a brief script of the role play before acting it out.

1. (buyer, jewelry vendor)

BUYER: You have been looking for an emerald necklace for a long time to give to your girlfriend, and finally you found one that is perfect! The only problem is that you're not sure the vendor is giving you a fair price; besides, you don't have the money. You would have to go into debt to pay for it. But it's so beautiful . . . what should you do?

VENDOR: Try to convince this man he's not going to find a necklace like this anywhere else—he should take advantage of your offer. You are even willing to let him have it for less money than it's actually worth.

2. (adult son or daughter, parent)

ADULT SON OR DAUGHTER: You have just moved away from home and it's a lot more difficult than you thought it would be to survive. Call your parent and tell him/her of your difficulties. Ask for more money.

PARENT: Your child has just moved away for the first time, and is having a tough time. Advise your child on the importance of learning to be financially responsible, even though it may be hard at first.

USING THE IDIOMS IN WRITING

E. Writing with Idioms

Write a short brochure based on the situation described below, using the idioms from this chapter.

A large bank has asked you to write a brochure that they will send to new credit applicants. In it, you must offer advice to help people realize the dangers of overusing their credit cards. Credit card debt is a big problem for many people who have not learned to properly manage their money. It is easy to get into the habit of continually buying on credit, always with a "pay later" attitude. When "later" comes, many find themselves unable to get out of debt. The bank you work for has begun an advertising campaign to encourage the responsible use of credit. They are planning to mail this brochure to every person who wants to get a credit card. Be sure to use the idioms from this chapter in your brochure.

F. Advertising with Idioms

Make up an advertisement for any type of product not advertised in the ads in this chapter, using one or more of the idioms you have just learned. Follow the steps listed below.

1. Choose a product or service that you would like to advertise.

2. Determine your audience—the people most likely to buy your product or service.

3. Determine what value(s) would appeal to that audience. How are you going to incorporate that value into your ad?

4. Make up a slogan, using one of the idioms from this chapter.

5. Decide what visual cues (pictures, etc.) will accompany the slogan.

6. Write the rest of the ad.

7. Present it to the class. Do you think this ad would appeal to the other members of your class?

Idioms

DROP IN

STAY IN TOUCH

COME ALIVE

KEEP SOMETHING BOTTLED UP

FLOOR SOMEONE

MAKE WAVES

OUT OF THIS WORLD

GET THE PICTURE

THE LAST WORD

TRAVEL IN THE WRONG CIRCLES

FAIRWEATHER FRIEND

EGG ON ONE'S FACE

I Learning the Idioms

WARMING UP

Complete the following activity and questions in pairs or small groups. Compare answers and discuss with your classmates.

1. Who (or what) are the biggest newsmakers in the world today? Ask five of your classmates about the people or events that attracted the most publicity in their countries within the past year. Then, in a small group of three to five students, make a list of the five biggest news stories around the world during the last year.

2. You must choose one of several newspaper articles to read on your break from classes. The headlines for each article are written below. Which article will you choose? Why? Ask your classmates which one they would read, and why.

WAR BREAKS OUT!

LOCH NESS MONSTER IS CAPTURED!

NUCLEAR SUBMARINES COLLIDE!

FAMOUS ACTRESS KILLED BY TV LOVER!

WORLD LEADERS MEET WITH MESSENGERS FROM ANOTHER PLANET!

CHILD GENIUS FINDS CURE FOR AIDS!

GIGANTIC EARTHQUAKE PREDICTED WITHIN ONE WEEK!

3. Do you think the media does a good, fair, or poor job of accurately reporting the news? How do you think news agencies decide what stories are the most important?

4. How do rumors get started? Can you remember a rumor you have heard about a celebrity? Did you believe it? Do you think rumors should ever be reported in the news?

GETTING TO KNOW THE IDIOMS

A. Listening for Understanding

Listen to the following radio talk show, hosted by Dixie Ditz.
Consider these questions as you listen to the program. Afterward,
discuss the answers with your classmates in pairs or small groups.

1. What is "True or False?" What does Dixie Ditz do on the show?

2. Describe the kind of outfit you think Madonna is going to wear during her next concert tour.

3. What did Brian, Jimmy, and Sara each want to know? What did Dixie tell them?

4. If you were a guest on Dixie's show, what would you ask?

5. Have you ever watched a TV talk show in the United States, such as "Phil Donahue," "Sally Jesse Raphael," "Geraldo!," or "Oprah Winfrey"? What kinds of issues were discussed? What were your impressions?

6. Are talk shows popular in your country? Are they similar to those in the United States? What would be some popular topics for discussion?

B. Identifying the Idioms

Next, read the script of the talk show to which you have just listened. Throughout the script you will find the idioms listed below. Underline the idioms, and number them on the list in the order in which you find them. Can you tell what they mean by how they are used?

_____ drop in

_____ travel in the wrong circles

_____ floor someone

_____ egg on one's face

_____ keep something bottled up

_____ stay in touch

_____ come alive

_____ the last word

_____ make waves

_____ get the picture

_____ out of this world

_____ fairweather friend

GIVE HER THE LAST WORD

"Hi! I'm Dixie Ditz, your favorite talk show hostess. It's nice of you to drop in this afternoon for "True or False?" the show that always has the last word! No matter how outrageous the rumors you've heard, I'll tell you if there's any truth to them. You give me your gossip; I'll let you know if you can believe it. This week I heard some fantastic stories that I just can't keep bottled up any longer! My guests have inquired about everything from Madonna to UFOs—get the picture? I'm sure you will love the show today, so let's get started!"

My first question comes from Cindy, in Oregon. Hi, Cindy, you're on the air!"

"Hi, Dixie. Is it true that Madonna is planning to show up on stage without any clothes on during her next concert tour?"

"Well, Madonna's outfits in the past have been pretty wild, but I have heard that she hired a new designer to create a completely different look for her. I don't know what it is, but I'm sure it will be out of this world; Madonna never fails to scandalize the public. No doubt there will be plenty of men in the audience who will suddenly come alive when she appears on stage.

"Next, I have a question from Brian, in Pennsylvania. Go ahead, Brian."

"Dixie, I was just wondering what you think of the rumor that Elvis Presley's fan club has stayed in touch with Presley's spirit by hiring a psychic to relay messages back and forth."

"Brian, if that is true, then Elvis Presley is a fairweather friend—it seems that the fan club hears from the dead singer only when the psychic collects her high fee as a 'celebrity messenger.' And in case you're interested, according to the hired psychic, Elvis is doing fine, but he misses his favorite guitar.

"Let's move on now to a question from Jimmy, from Alaska. Are you there, Jimmy?"

"Yeah, I'm here. I heard that at least one of the major tobacco companies in the United States owns marijuana fields in Mexico and recently has been making waves by suggesting that marijuana should be legalized. Is that true?"

"Don't believe it, Jimmy. I would be floored if our Congress ever seriously considered legalizing drug use, so even if the rumor were true (and it's not), marijuana will never be legal in this country.

"Sara from Louisiana is next. What's your question, Sara?"

"Hello, Dixie. Someone told me that a UFO crashed last month, and the bodies of the space aliens are being studied by the CIA. True or false?"

"Sara, I guess I travel in the wrong circles because I do not personally know any space aliens, and the CIA is very secretive about their operations. However, I don't believe the story. I think that people who report on visits from extraterrestrial beings usually end up with egg on their face when the stories are proved false.

"Well, that's all for today. Join me next week on "True or False?" when we discuss alligators living in the White House swimming pool, and whether there was really once a woman pope!"

C. Getting the Meaning

Notice the highlighted phrase in each of the following sentences. Pay attention to how the idiom is used, and try to guess its meaning. You may also refer to the preceding talk show. Write the meaning of the idiom on the line. The first one is done for you.

1. It was nice of you to come see us. Please **drop in** again if you're in the area!

   <u>To pay someone a short, informal visit .</u>

2. No matter what we argue about, you always have to **have the last word**.

   _____

3. Warren told me not to tell anyone, but I can't **keep it bottled up** another minute. Would you like to know what he said?

   _____

4. There's no way to escape from this prison. There are guards everywhere, an electric fence, vicious dogs, and searchlights. **Get the picture**?

   _____

5. There's a wonderful new exhibit at the art museum that you must see! Some of the paintings are **out of this world**!

   _____

6. David looked like he was going to fall asleep until his friends walked in. Then he suddenly **came alive**.

   _____

7. Don't forget me after I move away. Please **stay in touch**!

   _____

8. I've heard that Hollywood is full of **fairweather friends**. As long as you are successful, everyone wants to be with you. But if you run into some bad luck, you are suddenly alone.

   _____

9. The protesters were trying to **make waves** by yelling and throwing things during the president's speech.

   _____

10. I was **floored** when I heard they were getting married—I never would have imagined the two of them together!

_____

11. No, we weren't invited to the president's inaugural ball. I guess we **travel in the wrong circles**.

_____

12. Marty told everyone the play started at 8:00, but it really started at 7:00. Everyone missed half the show, and he **has egg on his face**.

_____

PRACTICING THE IDIOMS

D. Choosing the Best Answer

First, listen carefully to the following taped statements. Read the choices listed below for each statement you hear. Select the sentence that best relates to the original statement and circle the corresponding letter.

Next, guess if the statement you have just heard is true or just a rumor; circle T *if it is true, and* F *if it is false.*

1. T / F   a.   Michael Jordan's friends dropped in on him.
          b.   Michael Jordan kept his plans bottled up.
          c.   Michael Jordan's friends came alive at the press conference.

2. T / F   a.   That scene made people come alive.
          b.   Clark Gable had egg on his face.
          c.   Clark Gable was floored by the movie.

3. T / F   a.   King Louis XIV always got the last word.
          b.   His friends came alive when the king visited them.
          c.   His friends didn't like it when the king dropped in.

4. T / F   a.   She came alive when she was with her friends.
          b.   She stayed in touch with her friends.
          c.   She traveled in the wrong circles.

5. T / F   a.   Castro had egg on his face when the movie came out.
          b.   Critics said his performance was out of this world.
          c.   Castro was floored by the criticism of his movie.

6. T / F a. The reporter was a fairweather friend.
        b. The reporter got the picture.
        c. The director of the space program had egg on his face.

7. T / F a. The Saudi prince got the last word.
        b. The attorney said that husbands and wives are usually fairweather friends.
        c. Most marriage partners are out of this world.

8. T / F a. Napoleon got the last word.
        b. Napoleon kept the national anthem bottled up.
        c. The national anthem was out of this world.

9. T / F a. The royal couple traveled in the wrong circles.
        b. The Prince and Princess were floored when their marriage failed.
        c. The royal couple made waves when their separation was confirmed.

10. T / F a. Researchers can drop in on people who live far away.
        b. They get the picture when they talk to people who are far away.
        c. They can mentally stay in touch with people who are far away.

11. T / F a. The public was floored by the amazing story.
        b. The public made waves by discovering the scientist's brain.
        c. The public dropped in on the doctor in Kansas.

12. T / F a. Although the doctors got the picture, they did not reveal the king's true state.
        b. The king dropped in on his doctors to find out how he was doing.
        c. The doctors made waves by predicting the king would die.

E. Retelling the Story—Optional Activity

Read the script of the radio talk show on pages 186–187 again.
The sentences below refer to statements in that script. On the lines
below, restate the sentences, using the appropriate idiom in each
one. The first one is done for you.

1. Dixie Ditz was glad that her listeners could visit her show for a few moments.

   Dixie Ditz was happy that her listeners could drop in for a while.

2. "True or False?" is a show that always makes the final point in a controversial discussion.

3. Dixie heard some rumors that she had to tell her audience; she just couldn't keep them secret any longer.

4. Dixie mentioned a couple of the topics she would discuss, in hopes that her audience would understand that she had a very wide range of topics.

_____

5. Dixie said that Madonna's new look would be extraordinary.

_____

6. She said that there would probably be many men who would become excited upon seeing the famous star on stage.

_____

7. Brian asked if some of Elvis Presley's fans had maintained contact with the singer after his death.

_____

8. Dixie said that if it is true that the psychic relays messages to and from Presley, then it shows that Elvis only responds in a friendly manner when there is money involved.

_____

9. Another listener asked if a tobacco company was causing a commotion by proposing that marijuana be legalized.

_____

10. Dixie replied that she would be extremely surprised if such legislation were ever considered.

_____

11. Dixie admitted that she probably associates with the wrong group of people to find out for sure if a rumor about a UFO is true.

_____

12. She feels that anyone who tell stories about space aliens usually ends up feeling very embarrassed when the truth is discovered.

_____

F. Putting the Idioms into Practice

Read the beginning of the following newspaper articles. Then write an appropriate headline for each article, using the idiom given. Remember that headlines are usually written in "telegraph" style, rather than as a grammatical sentence.

Examples:

- *TWO-HEADED MONSTER HAS TWINS*
- *DONALD DUCK WINS PRESIDENTIAL ELECTION.*

1. **drop in**

   _____

   Eight years ago, Jack M. Tepper mysteriously disappeared. He was presumed dead after police found his abandoned truck with blood on the seat. However, yesterday afternoon, the same Mr. Tepper casually walked into his home, claiming he'd been gone for only an hour or two. Mr. Tepper's wife was . . . .

2. **fairweather friend**

   _____

   A well-known environmental activist has suddenly shifted her loyalty to the People over Trees movement, causing an uproar in the environmentalists' camp. Members of her former organization claim that the woman's defection was due to the fact that the leader of "People over Trees" had promised her fame and money. They also said that . . . .

3. **travel in the wrong circles**

   _____

   A seventeen-year-old honors student was shot and killed as she was walking with her boyfriend along a busy street. Police have speculated that the gunman was probably aiming at the girl's boyfriend, who is a known criminal. Just before the shooting occurred . . . .

4. **come alive**

Many people who gathered to hear the symphony orchestra were a bit surprised when the musicians opened their performance with a medley of rock and roll songs. The audience responded enthusiastically to the music by clapping their hands in rhythm, singing along, and even dancing in the aisles. The musicians were . . . .

5. **egg on one's face**

Dr. Christopher Sexton, a prominent medical researcher, has withdrawn his name from consideration for the Nobel Prize in medicine. Dr. Sexton achieved notoriety when he claimed that, after extensive testing, he had found a cure for cancer. However, after one of Dr. Sexton's assistants revealed that the results of his clinical trials were falsified, Dr. Sexton admitted that he had lied. He said . . . .

6. **make waves**

A housewife with two children has provoked a lot of media attention after she claimed to have been Marilyn Monroe in a previous life. She said that she made the discovery through hypnosis. The man responsible for hypnotizing the woman says that . . . .

7. **get the last word**

The two vice-presidential candidates held their last formal debate earlier today, and once again, the issues of education and health care became the focus of their discussion. Although the Democratic candidate seemed well prepared with the facts, his Republican counterpart insisted on making the final point on each question. A poll taken after the debate showed . . . .

8. **get the picture**

Speaking to a large crowd of concerned students, a group of scientists projected shocking and graphic images of what the world will look like in 100 years if we continue to destroy the earth's natural resources. Obviously comprehending the magnitude of the problem, the audience pledged its support to the organization the scientists represented. A discussion followed . . . .

9. **keep something bottled up**

Film star Zella Fenn revealed today that she and film producer Carl Johnson have been married for over one year, and they are expecting their first child in May. "We felt we couldn't keep it a secret any longer," said Ms. Fenn, "but at the time it was necessary because . . . ."

10. **out of this world**

The largest diamond known to man was just found in an abandoned mine in South Africa. The man who found the record-breaking diamond was very excited about his discovery, saying it was simply unbelievable! The diamond weighed . . . .

11. **stay in touch**

When Doug Spears moved away from his childhood home where he had been a neighbor and friend of Irene Feldman, they promised to write each other and call occasionally. However, neither of them expected that more than fifty years later, they would be getting married! It is a second marriage for both, but they are as excited as they were . . . .

12. **floor someone**

When local resident Victor O'Hara stopped to help a stranded motorist who was struggling with a flat tire, he got one of the biggest surprises of his life. The woman was Lauren Bishop, the newly crowned Miss Universe. The beauty queen was very grateful for his help, and promised . . . .

II Finding the Idioms in Ads

INTERPRETING THE ADS

Look at the following advertisements. First determine what is being advertised and what idiom is featured in the ad. Review the meaning of the idiom. Then answer the questions corresponding to each ad.

1. How are Fantastic Foods different from most other packaged foods?

2. What does this company want you to understand?

3. How does the picture of the containers of food contribute to the meaning of the idiom?

1. "They said it couldn't be done."
   What does "it" refer to?

2. Why would Simply Eggs want to
   spin the cholesterol out of eggs?
   What is cholesterol?

3. Did Simply Eggs accomplish what
   others said was impossible?

4. Why do "they have egg on their
   face"?

1. What do you see in the picture?
   Where is this famous mountain
   located? The weather around this
   mountain is known to be quite
   temperamental; most of the time
   it is covered with clouds, but
   occasionally there is "fair weather" and it can be seen. How
   does the picture relate to the
   idiom?

2. Why does the company say that
   it is not a fairweather friend?

1. Have you ever played Scrabble? Do you know what kind of a game it is?

2. Why is this edition of Scrabble special? What do you think an ordinary version of the game looks like?

3. Why do the advertisers say that this is "the last word" in word games? What does that mean?

4. Who do you think would buy this edition of Scrabble?

1. Where is this hotel located?

2. In what way is the hotel "making waves"?

Introducing the hotel that's making waves on the Chicago River. The Stouffer Rivière Hotel.

The Stouffer Rivière Hotel is located at the corner of State Street and Wacker Drive, between The Loop and The Magnificent Mile. Our convenient location puts you in the center of the city's lively downtown area and offers you the spectacular city, lake, and river views unique to our address at One West Wacker Drive.

During your stay, wake up to complimentary coffee and newspaper, enjoy exciting cuisine in our two restaurants or 24-hour room service, unwind in our complimentary pool and health club, or be pampered in our Club Floor accommodations.

Elegant and comfortable, the Stouffer Rivière Hotel provides a standard of service you thought had disappeared forever.

Whether you are here on business, personal getaway, or both, experience the winning combination of luxury and location. Call your travel agent or 1•800•HOTELS•1.

STOUFFER RIVIERE HOTEL
CHICAGO, IL

STOUFFER HOTELS ▪ RESORTS *SHR*

A Nestlé Company

© 1992 Stouffer Hotel Company

1. Palm Springs is in southern California, near Los Angeles. What do you think the climate is like in Palm Springs?

2. Palm Springs has a number of features for which it is famous, such as its golf courses. Can you tell from the picture what another of its features is?

3. Can you explain the literal as well as the idiomatic meaning of "drop in during the week"?

THINKING ABOUT THE ADS

Review the ads from this chapter. Based on the messages contained in the ads, choose the one that you think best illustrates American cultural values. Complete statements one through four based on that ad.

1. This ad would appeal to an American audience because . . . .

2. It is important to many Americans to . . . .

3. Other examples in American life that show how Americans feel about this issue or value are . . . .

4. This ad would/would not appeal to an audience from my country because . . . .

5. The ad that I liked the best is . . . .

6. The ad that made the best use of an idiom is . . . because . . . .

III Using the Idioms

USING THE IDIOMS IN SPEECH

A. One-minute Speech

Write a brief outline before presenting your one-minute speech to your classmates. Be sure to use the idioms from this chapter in your speech.

Make up a truly outrageous rumor about one or more of the celebrities listed below. Your rumor may or may not have any truth at all to it; be creative!

King Kong	**Sean Connery**
Charlie Chaplin	**Michael Jordan**
Cindy Crawford	**Monica Seles**
Madonna	**Paul McCartney**
Dracula	**Elizabeth Taylor**
Boris Yeltsin	**Minnie Mouse**

B. Group Discussion

Participate in the following discussion, using the idioms from this chapter.

Your group is representing a dancer who appeared as the "double" for a famous actress in a movie about a woman who wins a prestigious dance award. The problem is that the production company failed to give the dancer credit for her performance in the movie, allowing audiences to believe that the actress had done her own dancing scenes. At first, the dancer kept quiet about her role, but when the media acclaimed the actress's dancing as "phenomenal," she—the *real* dancer—decided to do something about it. Discuss the following with your group:

- Explain why the dancer waited so long to tell anyone about her role in the movie.

- What you can do to make the production company tell the truth about the dancing scenes.

- The actress will be very embarrassed to have the truth come out so late, and it may damage her career. This is a sensitive issue, particularly because she has been very helpful to the dancer in securing other roles in movies. Should you do anything to protect the actress from negative publicity?

C. Debate: Adoption

Read the situation and choose to defend either side of the following question: Should the girl stay with her adoptive parents or go to her birth parents? *Before you begin, jot down the arguments supporting your position. Remember to use as many of the idioms from this chapter as you can.*

A baby girl was adopted at birth by a loving couple who couldn't have any children of their own. The baby's birth mother was unmarried, had recently ended her relationship with the child's birth father, and thought it best to give the girl up for adoption. However, several months after agreeing to the adoption, the birth mother changed her mind and renewed her relationship with her boyfriend. Together they decided that they wanted their daughter back. Subsequently they got married, and they continued their fight to regain their baby girl. Now there were two sets of parents who loved the girl and wanted her to live with them. By the time the case went to trial, the girl was two years old and had known only her adoptive parents. Nevertheless, the birth parents believed they had been cheated and that their daughter would be better off with them.

D. Role Plays

Imagine yourself in one of the situations described below. Act it out with another member of your class, using as many idioms from this chapter as you can in your conversation. You and your partner may want to write a brief script of the role play before acting it out.

1. (woman client, psychic)

WOMAN: Your husband has been dead for several years. You would like to get married again, but you feel that you ought to get the approval of your husband's spirit first. Ask the psychic to help you contact your dead husband so you can ask him.

PSYCHIC: A woman wants you to find her dead husband's spirit so she can ask him if he likes the man his wife is dating. You must speak on behalf of the dead husband. Tell her that her husband doesn't think her current boyfriend is good for her.

2. (Dixie Ditz, a guest on her show)

GUEST: Think of three or four questions to ask Dixie Ditz. Have you heard any rumors lately? If not, then make them up, and ask Dixie!

DIXIE: As always, you will tell your guests if there is any truth to the rumors they have heard. Answer your guest's questions about the wild and crazy things people might or might not have done.

USING THE IDIOMS IN WRITING

E. Writing with Idioms

Three different stories have been started for you below. Choose one of the story openings and write it on a separate piece of paper. Then write one paragraph to continue the story. Next, exchange your story with one of your classmates. Each of you will write one more paragraph and then exchange stories once again (either with your original partner or with someone new). Be sure to use at least one of the idioms from this chapter in each paragraph.

1. In a remote part of Antarctica, a scientist discovered a frozen dinosaur egg. The scientist predicted the egg would hatch if it were allowed to thaw.

2. One day I decided to go riding in a spaceship.

3. Bobby simply couldn't believe that he had really been sleepwalking in the park with no clothes on.

F. Advertising with Idioms

Make up an advertisement for any type of product not *advertised in the ads in this chapter, using one or more of the idioms you have just learned. Follow the steps listed below.*

1. Choose a product or service that you would like to advertise.

2. Determine your audience—the people most likely to buy your product or service.

3. Determine what value(s) would appeal to that audience. How are you going to incorporate that value into your ad?

4. Make up a slogan, using one of the idioms from this chapter.

5. Decide what visual cues (pictures, etc.) will accompany the slogan.

6. Write the rest of the ad.

7. Present it to the class. Do you think this ad would appeal to the other members of your class?

ACHIEVING SUCCESS

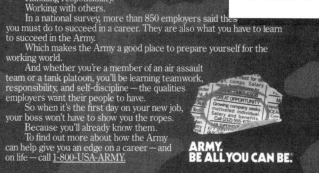

Before you start your career,
it pays to learn the ropes.

Making decisions.
Handling responsibility.
Working with others.
In a national survey, more than 850 employers said these
you must do to succeed in a career. They are also what you have to learn
to succeed in the Army.
Which makes the Army a good place to prepare yourself for the
working world.
And whether you're a member of an air assault
team or a tank platoon, you'll be learning teamwork,
responsibility, and self-discipline — the qualities
employers want their people to have.
So when it's the first day on your new job,
your boss won't have to show you the ropes.
Because you'll already know them.
To find out more about how the Army
can help give you an edge on a career — and
on life — call 1-800-USA-ARMY.

**ARMY.
BE ALL YOU CAN BE.**

Idioms

GET ROLLING

GET ONE'S GEARS TURNING

LEARN THE ROPES

NO SWEAT

GO BY THE BOOK

TO THE LETTER

WORTH ONE'S SALT

STACK UP

SNOWED UNDER

GIVE SOMEONE THE RUNAROUND

MIDDLE-OF-THE-ROAD

GO BELLY-UP

I Learning the Idioms

WARMING UP

If you were to own and operate your own business, what type of business would it be? How would you make sure it was successful? In small groups, discuss how you would design, market, and sell an original product or service. Follow the steps listed below.

1. First decide what type of business you would like to operate. Use your imagination; you could provide robots to do people's housework, complete homework for lazy students, sell vacations to another planet, offer a dating service, and so on. Whatever it is, you must be confident that it is something the public needs or wants.

   - If you are selling a product, be ready to describe it in detail and tell why people would want to buy it.

   - If it is a service, prepare to explain exactly what you will do for your customers.

2. Next, create a simple advertisement for your business that will immediately attract the attention of consumers. You may draw a picture if you like, think of a clever slogan, or simply use big, bold letters.

3. Finally, you must try to sell your group's product or service to your classmates. Walk around the classroom, and talk to your fellow consumers about your group's business. Try to convince them to buy from you. Your goal is to make as many sales as you can.

4. You (individually) may make only one purchase from other members of the class, so choose carefully. (You *cannot* buy your own product.) Make sure you know what all your options are before you buy. Once you place an order with someone, it is final. There are no returns or exchanges.

5. At the end of the activity, see who has the most customers. Why did this person sell more than anyone else? Was it the product or service, the advertising, or the personality of the salesperson that was most influential?

If you were advising someone on starting his/her own business, what would you say? Discuss it with two or three other members of your group, and write down three to five suggestions you might give. Compare your list with that of other groups.

GETTING TO KNOW THE IDIOMS

A. Listening for Understanding

Listen to the following excerpt from a book on how to operate a successful business. Consider these questions as you listen to the excerpt. Afterward, discuss the answers with your classmates in pairs or small groups.

1. What do you need to do to learn the ropes?

2. In what way will you be at an advantage if you get your gears turning?

3. At what point should you get rolling?

4. How should your business compare with your competitors'?

5. What can you do to make sure the customer is king?

6. What element is needed sometimes more than any other to make things work?

B. Identifying the Idioms

Next, read the book excerpt to which you have just listened.
Throughout the excerpt you will find the idioms listed below.
Underline the idioms, and number them on the list in the order in
which you find them. Can you tell what they mean by how they are
used?

_____ **get rolling**   _____ **give someone the runaround**

_____ **no sweat**   _____ **learn the ropes**

_____ **snowed under**   _____ **get one's gears turning**

_____ **worth one's salt**   _____ **go by the book**

_____ **middle-of-the-road**   _____ **to the letter**

_____ **stack up**   _____ **go belly-up**

LEARNING THE ROPES

Mr. Sam Leland, business executive and author of the best-selling book How to Be Your Own Boss offers some advice for ambitious entrepreneurs.

.1. Learn the ropes. Starting your own business is never easy. There is much that you need to know, and you must assume that you will make some mistakes. Many crucial business errors can be avoided, however. The first and most important thing to do is make sure you know as much as possible about your business and what will make it profitable before you open your doors.

.2. Get your gears turning. What will sell in today's overcrowded market is a superior product at a lower cost. Never stop thinking about how to improve your product or service; think about it at dinner, in the shower, while you're asleep. Be creative. Don't always go by the book. If you can think of a way to do things better than they've always been done, do it! (Remember, however, that some rules can't be broken; be sure to follow all legal requirements and regulations to the letter.)

.3. Get rolling. Experience is always the best teacher, so get started as soon as possible. Don't wait for everything to be perfect before you open your doors. Your business will continue to expand and improve as you learn what your clients want.

.4. Always be aware of your competition. How does your product or service stack up? Remember that to stay in business you always have to be a little bit better than the other guys. No businessman worth his salt would be content with a middle-of-the-road product or sales performance. You simply can't afford to be average. If you do not remain competitive, your business will not survive. You will go belly-up before you know it.

.5. Keep in mind that the customer is king. Do everything you can to satisfy your client, no matter what it takes. Learn to say, "No sweat!" to any request. Find a way to make it happen. Even when you get snowed under by phone calls, bills, and work orders, you must treat your customers with

dignity and respect. Tell them you value their patronage, and above all, never give them the runaround. Be honest with them, and they will remain loyal to you. If they are dissatisfied, work harder than ever to please them. A happy customer is your best advertisement.

.6. Don't get discouraged. It's possible that in spite of your best efforts, your business may fail anyway. If I had given up after my first failed attempt, I wouldn't be where I am today. Sometimes luck is largely responsible for success, so my final words to you are, Good luck!

C. Getting the Meaning

Notice the highlighted phrase in each of the following sentences. Pay attention to how the idiom is used, and try to guess its meaning. You may also refer to the preceding excerpt. Write the meaning of the idiom on the line. The first one is done for you.

1. They say the first year of law school is really hard, but I'm sure once you **learn the ropes,** you'll do fine.

   to learn how things are done

2. I think Scott is going to be an inventor when he grows up. He tries to find creative solutions to every little thing that goes wrong; he's always **got his gears turning.**

3. It's especially important for the police to **go by the book.** Law and order depends on having officers who don't break the rules.

4. I followed your recipe **to the letter,** but my bread came out flat and hard. What do you think happened?

_____

5. Come on! Quit wasting time! Let's **get rolling!**

_____

6. Pepsi-Cola often runs taste tests to see how their soft drink **stacks up** against Coke.

_____

7. I guess I'm going to have to fire my secretary. I've given her repeated warnings, but she still isn't **worth her salt.**

_____

8. Although Jamie's marks have improved somewhat, her reading skills remain merely **middle of the road.**

_____

9. The restaurant lasted for only two months before it **went belly-up.** They just didn't have enough customers to make any money.

_____

10. "Do you think you can have this done by the end of the week?"

    "**No sweat!** In fact, I'll have it ready by tomorrow morning."

_____

11. Look at my desk! I've got enough paperwork to last me a month. I'm **snowed under!**

_____

12. I went to the Social Security office to get the forms, but they just **gave me the runaround.** They sent me to three different places before I finally got what I needed.

_____

PRACTICING THE IDIOMS

D. Choosing the Best Answer

Listen carefully to the following taped statements. Read the choices listed below for each statement you hear. Select the sentence that best relates to the original statement, and circle the corresponding letter.

1. a. In order to play cricket, you must be tied to your teammates.
    b. In order to play cricket, you must learn the rules of the game.

2. a. We'll have to postpone the party.
    b. We should try to figure out a theme.

3. a. Ms. Telly is strict and inflexible.
    b. Ms. Telly reads from the textbook a lot.

4. a. You must complete your tasks exactly as outlined.
    b. You must write a letter indicating when you have completed your tasks.

5. a. The concrete will roll onto the house if it is poured now.
    b. No one can get started until the strike is over.

6. a. This kind is as good as the shampoo in the salon.
    b. The salon shampoo is clearly better because it costs more.

7. a. Trevor has lost jobs because he doesn't have enough salt.
    b. Trevor's work is not worth what he is paid.

8. a. The team has been playing its games in the street.
    b. They have won as many games as they've lost.

9. a. We will go out of business if we lower our prices again.
    b. Our prices are about to go up again.

10. a. My mechanic doesn't perspire much when he's working.
    b. My mechanic can fix anything easily.

11. a. It snows too much here!
    b. I've got too much to do!

12. a. My lawyer can help you get immediate answers.
    b. You should go to several different sources to make sure you get what you need.

E. Retelling the Story—Optional Activity

Read the excerpt from Mr. Leland's book on pages 206–207 again.
The sentences below refer to statements in that excerpt. On the lines
below, restate the sentences, using the appropriate idiom in each
one. The first one is done for you.

1. The first thing you should do if you want to start your own business is learn what to do and how to do it.

    Before you start your own business, you should learn the ropes.

2. Secondly, you should begin to think creatively about what you can do to be better than your competitors.

    _____

3. You should not necessarily be rigid and inflexible in getting things done.

    _____

4. However, you should always follow government regulations precisely.

    _____

5. Get started as soon as possible.

    _____

6. You should constantly be aware of how your product or service compares with others like it.

    _____

7. A successful businessperson is one who is worth the salary he or she makes.

    _____

8. Never be satisfied with being simply average.

    _____

9. Your business will go bankrupt if it is not competitive.

    _____

10. You should always be able to tell your customers that you can meet their requests without any problem.

    _____

11. You may at times become overwhelmed by the work you have, but you should still treat your customers well.

_____

12. Your customers will not appreciate it if you give them excuses or refer them elsewhere to get their work done.

_____

F. **Putting the Idioms into Practice**

You are a counselor at an English school in a large American city. Students from all over the world are enrolled in your school, and it is your job to help them with any problems they may encounter while they are there. As you read the following situations, decide what advice would be most appropriate. Fill in the blanks with the idioms listed below. Remember to change the idioms as needed to fit the sentences.

get rolling	**get the runaround**
no sweat	**learn the ropes**
snowed under	**get one's gears turning**
worth one's salt	**go by the book**
middle-of-the-road	**to the letter**
stack up	**go belly-up**

1. Yumi Kikuchi just arrived yesterday. She is anxious and nervous because she doesn't know how to get around the school or what will be expected of her in her classes. You know she will do fine once she learns how things are done around here. Tell her not to worry; soon she will

_____ .

2. Rosa Fernández is usually very involved in school activities, and she has agreed to plan a party for the students who are leaving. However, she is feeling over-whelmed because she also has to study for the TOEFL exam and has two major writing assignments to complete as well. Tell her she shouldn't have tried to do so much at the same time; it's her own fault that she is

_____ .

3. Urs Schmidt has been assigned to write a story about life in the future for his advanced writing class. He just can't think of any interesting ideas to start his story. Tell him to be creative and let his mind go; he's got to

_____ .

4. Eric Swenson needs a housing application for Lakeview College. He asks if you could get one for him. You have an ample supply in your desk, so it's absolutely no problem. You answer,

_____ .

5. Laura Sandoval wants to get into a prestigious American university, but her grades at the school and her TOEFL scores have been merely average. Tell her she needs to study more; the university will not accept students with marks that are

_____ .

6. Harvey Wu has been in the United States for seven years and wants to get a green card. He is suspicious of government bureaucracy and is trying to find out if there is an easier and quicker way to get approval for his request. (His family has plenty of money.) You explain that unless he wants to risk getting in trouble, he had better strictly follow all government regulations. He should definitely

_____ .

7. Nicole Petri's grammar class begins in about twenty minutes, and she hasn't done her homework assignment yet. You advise her to

_____ .

8. You get a phone call from a student in Saudi Arabia who wants information on your school. He would like to compare your program to various others that are offered in different cities throughout the United States. You promise to send him a brochure that shows how your program

_____ .

9. Kiri Mantovani has been trying to extend her visa so she can stay longer in the United States. However, every time she has tried to get the right forms to fill out, she has been sent to a different department or office, and she still doesn't have what she needs. Tell her you'll take care of it for her; you are sorry that she

_____ .

10. You got a phone call today from the owner of a bookstore who occasionally employs students from your school who need work. He said that Pierre Renard, who has been working there for a couple of weeks, is inefficient, lazy, and always late to work. He asks you what he should do about it. You tell him that he should not feel responsible for keeping an employee who is not

_____ .

11. Another student who has a job at a small business in the community is concerned because she hasn't been paid in over a month. She thinks the owner is having financial difficulties. Tell her to find another job as soon as possible; it sounds like the business is about to

_____ .

12. Georges Perrine, a new student, turned in his class registration this morning, but it is incomplete and full of errors. Call him into your office and make sure he answers every question exactly as he is supposed to. Tell him to fill in each blank

_____ .

II Finding the Idioms in Ads

INTERPRETING THE ADS

Look at the following advertisements. First determine what is being advertised and what idiom is featured in the ad. Review the meaning of the idiom. Then answer the questions corresponding to each ad.

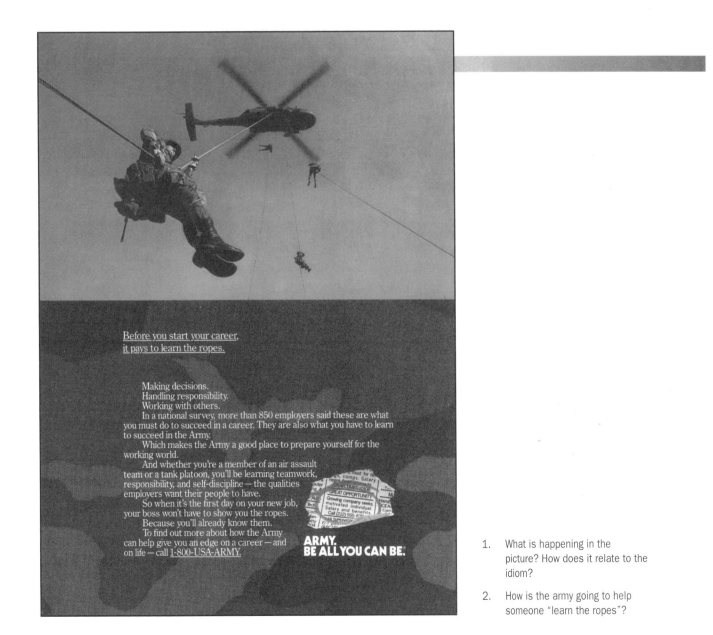

Before you start your career, it pays to learn the ropes.

Making decisions.
Handling responsibility.
Working with others.
In a national survey, more than 850 employers said these are what you must do to succeed in a career. They are also what you have to learn to succeed in the Army.
Which makes the Army a good place to prepare yourself for the working world.
And whether you're a member of an air assault team or a tank platoon, you'll be learning teamwork, responsibility, and self-discipline — the qualities employers want their people to have.
So when it's the first day on your new job, your boss won't have to show you the ropes.
Because you'll already know them.
To find out more about how the Army can help give you an edge on a career — and on life — call 1-800-USA-ARMY.

ARMY.
BE ALL YOU CAN BE.

1. What is happening in the picture? How does it relate to the idiom?

2. How is the army going to help someone "learn the ropes"?

1. How can Chevron gasoline help your car last longer?

2. How can using another brand of gasoline cause your investment to "go belly-up"?

3. How does the picture fit in with the ad's message?

Don't let your investment go belly-up.

It used to happen every year or two.
Your family would get a new car. But these days, cars cost more.
$17,000 on average. And people are keeping them longer.
So consider this. The wrong gasoline
could be the worst thing that ever happens to your car.
It can leave deposits that clog fuel injectors and cripple valves.
Only Chevron has Techroline,®
the special additive that helps keep your intake system clean.
And your car running like it should.
That's why Chevron is one of the best ways
to maintain your car's value. Though, we're sorry to say,
it can't bring back that new car smell.

Chevron

Simply **Smarter**

When it comes to safety features, compromise is quite possibly the only thing you won't find in the all-new 1992 Toyota Camry. That's why a driver-side air bag* is standard on every single Camry model. More high-strength tensile steel was added through-out the entire body to enhance rigidity, ride and handling. Plus, stopping power has been dramatically improved, with enlarged rotor size and brake pad volume. All Camrys even offer an optional Anti-lock Brake System (ABS).

To reduce eyestrain, the headlamps are brighter, and many of the controls are now closer to the driver's hands. But even with all these changes, Camry's legend-ary reputation for quality was left firmly intact. So, don't strad-dle the line where safety is concerned, drive the all-new un-compromising 1992 Toyota Camry.

WHEN IT COMES TO SAFETY, THE LAST PLACE YOU WANT TO BE IS MIDDLE OF THE ROAD.

THE ALL-NEW 1992 CAMRY.
WE JUST COULDN'T LEAVE WELL ENOUGH ALONE.

"I love what you do for me."
TOYOTA

*Camry features a driver-side air bag Supplemental Restraint System (SRS) which activates in a front-end accident of enough magnitude to inflate the bag. In a moderate collision, primary protection is provided by the 3-point shoulder and lap belt system, and the air bag may not inflate. So, safety belts should be worn at all times by all occupants. Call 1-800-GO-TOYOTA for a brochure and location of your nearest dealer. Get More From Life...Buckle Up! © 1991 Toyota Motor Sales, U.S.A., Inc.

1. Why shouldn't people drive in the middle of the road?

2. Explain what Toyota means by "When it comes to safety, the last place you want to be is middle of the road"?

3. The last line of text in this ad uses anoth-er idiom, "straddle the line." Do you know what that means? How does that fit in with the idiom "middle of the road"?

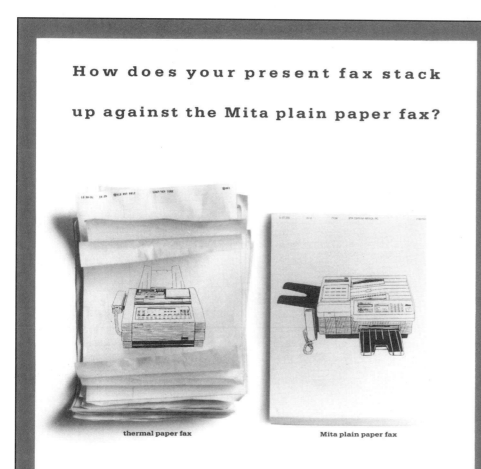

How does your present fax stack up against the Mita plain paper fax?

thermal paper fax   Mita plain paper fax

If the way your thermal faxes curl up is getting hard to handle, get a Mita plain paper fax machine instead ■ A Mita plain paper fax has a resolution of 400 x 400 dots-per-inch, so your images come out as good as if you'd printed them on a laser printer ■ They won't fade or smudge like thermal faxes ■ And with its expandable memory there may not be another fax machine in the world that can stack up to it ■ For more information on Mita's full line of plain paper fax machines, call 1-800-ABC-MITA.

[the image specialist]™

© 1992 MITA COPYSTAR AMERICA, INC.

1. What does the picture show? How are the two stacks of paper different?

2. The expression "to stack up" is used both literally and idiomatically in this ad. Can you explain?

1. How is Bank of America going to help the economy get rolling?

2. Is the sentence "We thought we'd give it a push" used literally or figuratively in this ad? Can you explain?

THINKING ABOUT THE ADS

Review the ads from this chapter. Based on the messages contained in the ads, choose the one that you think best illustrates American cultural values. Complete statements one through four based on that ad.

1. This ad would appeal to an American audience because . . . .

2. It is important to many Americans to . . . .

3. Other examples in American life that show how Americans feel about this issue or value are . . . .

4. This ad would/would not appeal to an audience from my country because . . . .

5. The ad that I liked the best is . . . .

6. The ad that made the best use of an idiom is . . . because . . . .

III Using the Idioms

USING THE IDIOMS IN SPEECH

A. One-minute Speech

Write a brief outline before presenting your one-minute speech to your classmates. Be sure to use the idioms from this chapter in your speech.

Imagine you have been taken back in time to the year 1875 for a special mission. Thomas Edison, the great American inventor, is discouraged and is about to give up. He has devoted all his spare time to research, and although he has had a little success, most of his attempts have ended in failure. You know that eventually he will invent the phonograph, the electric light bulb, and over a thousand other practical inventions; but *he* doesn't know that, and right now he feels that his efforts are largely wasted. It is your job to convince him to keep trying and to not give up. What will you say to him?

B. Group Discussion

Participate in the following discussion, using the idioms from this chapter.

Most students, from time to time, imagine how they would do things differently if *they* were the teacher. Well, now it's your turn to say what you think. How would *you* run *your* classroom? What kind of teacher would you be? Discuss the following questions with the other members of your group:

- Do you think a teacher should be strict or flexible?

- Are there certain classroom rules you believe should be rigid and nonnegotiable?

- How would you motivate your students to think creatively?

- How much homework is appropriate?

- Do you think a class should be easy enough for anyone to pass without much effort?

- If you were the teacher, how would your class compare to classes taught by other teachers?

- What do you think should be done about ineffective teachers?

C. Debate: English Only

Read the situation and choose to defend either side of the following question: Should election materials be printed in English only, or should minority groups be allowed to vote in their own languages? *Before you begin, jot down the arguments supporting your position. Remember to use as many of the idioms from this chapter as you can.*

According to law, in areas where more than five percent of the population speaks a minority language, the citizens in that area have the right to register and vote in their native tongue. Those who are in favor of this law claim that voting is the right of *all* citizens, and that in order to be properly informed on the issues, citizens should have election materials available in their own languages. They say to do otherwise would be to discriminate against a minority group.

However, many Americans oppose this law. They say that it constitutes a significant and unnecessary expense to print the same materials in several different languages. They also point out that English is the official language of the United States, and that by not learning to communicate in English, minorities exclude themselves from fully participating in American life.

D. Role Plays

Imagine yourself in one of the situations described below. Act it out with another member of your class, using as many idioms from this chapter as you can in your conversation. You and your partner may want to write a brief script of the role play before acting it out.

1. (patient in a large hospital, nurse)

PATIENT: You have just been admitted to the hospital with a very serious illness. The doctors in this hospital all seem to be overworked and haven't given you the time or attention you think you need. You are continually referred to someone else to get your questions answered. You are very concerned that you're not getting the appropriate treatment. Talk to the nurse about your concerns.

NURSE: You can certainly understand why this patient is worried; this is a very large and busy hospital, and until the patients figure out the routine, it can be a bit overwhelming. However, the doctors here are all very competent, and you are confident that this patient will receive the best care available. Try to reassure the patient.

2. (new employee, old employee)

NEW EMPLOYEE: Today is your first day at your new job. You reported to work early so you could start right away, but the office is in a state of total confusion. No one seems to be in charge, and everyone is giving you conflicting orders. You thought this would be a good opportunity for you, but if this is how this business is run, you imagine it cannot survive for very long. What should you do?

OLD EMPLOYEE: You can tell this person is new and obviously doesn't know how things are done around here. The first day is always difficult for new employees, but soon they understand how this office works, and everything is fine. Once they get going on a few of their own projects, they find that fulfilling their responsibilities is no problem. They just have to think creatively and not worry so much about following the rules, since no one does. Tell the new employee to ask you for help; otherwise, it may be somewhat frustrating because people here tend to just refer questions to someone else. In spite of how it appears, this company is doing much better than its competitors. Soon the new employee will love it as much as the rest of you do.

USING THE IDIOMS IN WRITING

E. Writing with Idioms

Write a letter based on the situation described below, using the idioms from this chapter.

Listed below are five common excuses that people use when they quit or give up. Think of something you have had difficulty doing or completing in the past (for example, a class, a job, travel away from home, joining a club). Did you use any of the excuses listed to keep from finishing? Which ones?

Interview a classmate about the situations in which he/she has quit or given up in the past. Then write a letter to your classmate encouraging the student to not give up.

Excuses:

- It's too hard!
- I don't have time.
- Someone else could do it better.
- I'm afraid of failure.
- I will be criticized.

F. Advertising with Idioms

Make up an advertisement for any type of product not *advertised in the ads in this chapter, using one or more of the idioms you have just learned. Follow the steps listed below.*

1. Choose a product or service that you would like to advertise.
2. Determine your audience—the people most likely to buy your product or service.
3. Determine what value(s) would appeal to that audience. How are you going to incorporate that value into your ad?
4. Make up a slogan, using one of the idioms from this chapter.
5. Decide what visual cues (pictures, etc.) will accompany the slogan.
6. Write the rest of the ad.
7. Present it to the class. Do you think this ad would appeal to the other members of your class?

APPENDIXES

GLOSSARY

Ahead of one's time (Ch. 4): new or revolutionary in concept; an idea that is at first met with resistance and doubt and is later widely accepted.
Example: *Leonardo da Vinci was ahead of his time when he made diagrams of flying machines based on true principles of aerodynamics.*

At one's feet (or right at one's feet) (Ch. 8): readily available and easily accessible.
Example: *We could build an entire resort on this land. Think of the possibilities right at our feet!*

Bend over backwards (Ch. 6): to make an extreme effort.
You would bend over backwards *for* someone; don't try to insert anything between *over* and *backwards*.
Example: *That waitress is bending over backwards for those people but they are still not satisfied.*

Beneath one (Ch. 8): inferior to one's usual standards.
This phrase has a somewhat negative connotation, so you probably would *not* use it in the first person. For example, *this car is beneath me* would imply that you are a snob.
Example: *Mr. Meyers only eats at the finest restaurants. Fast-food places are beneath him.*

Bite off more than one can chew (Ch. 5): to try to do more than one is capable of.
Example: *I'm taking too many classes this quarter; I think I bit off more than I can chew.*

Black and white (Ch. 1): To have two sides that are extremes: right and wrong, or good and bad, with nothing in between. Things can only be *black and white* if they have two sides to them; thus, concrete nouns (a house, a person, or a river) are not usually described as black and white, but issues, opinions, or ideas often are. This phrase is used as an adjective.
Example: *In my mind, the issue of abortion is black and white.*

Blow it (or to blow something) (Ch. 3): to make a big mistake; to ruin one's chances; to waste one's opportunities or money.
Example: *I should have told Mr. Tyson I could start work immediately, but I blew it! Now he's hired someone else.*
You may substitute *it* with another noun.
Example: *I'll give you twenty dollars if you promise not to blow your money on candy.*

Bounce a check (Ch. 10): to write a check without having sufficient money in one's account to cover it.
You cannot bounce a check *to* or *from* someone as you would bounce a ball.
Example: *The bank notified me that I had bounced three checks last month.*

Breathing room (Ch. 2): to have freedom from excessive control of one's time and attention.
This idiom is often used with *some*, or in the negative.
Example: *I can't get any work done with you talking to me all the time. Give me some breathing room!*

Bring to one's feet (Ch. 4): to provoke cheers and applause from a standing audience.
Example: *The appearance of their leader brought the union members to their feet.*
This idiom is sometimes used figuratively to indicate enthusiastic approval of someone or something.
Example: *The birth of the king and queen's first son brought the country to its feet.*

Bring to one's knees (Ch. 5): to incapacitate; to severely weaken the power of someone; to humiliate or humble someone.
The object always immediately follows *bring*; make sure that the possessive adjective agrees with that object.
Example: *The lawsuit brought the actress to her knees; it was a long time before she worked again.*

Call the shots (Ch. 7): to make the decisions; to be in charge.
Don't try to change *the* to a possessive adjective.
Example: *I don't care what you think; I'm calling the shots now.*

Catch one's eye (Ch. 8): to attract one's attention.
Example: *The brown puppy at the pet store caught my eye.*

Change one's tune (Ch. 1): To change how one feels or what one says about a particular issue.
Example: *She said she hated the book until she found out I was the author. Then she changed her tune.*

Cheap shot (or take a cheap shot) (Ch. 9): an unfair and unsporting statement made about someone.
This phrase is also used to describe aggressive physical contact that is unsporting. For example, if a boxer hits his opponent in the back, it might be called a *cheap shot.*
Example: *The newspaper said that the congressman's portrayal of his opponent as a criminal was a cheap shot. In reality, her police record consisted of one arrest when she was protesting for civil rights as a college student.*

Clear the air (Ch. 9): to settle differences; to remove the bad feelings and tension felt after an argument or disagreement.
Example: *Ed seems to think that after all of our arguments over the new house, bringing me some flowers will clear the air.*

Come alive (Ch. 11): to suddenly become lively and energetic, particularly just after one has been inattentive, indifferent, or bored.
Example: *Mark didn't come alive until they started talking about surfing.*

Corporate ladder (Ch. 7): the series of promotions and advancements required to rise to the top in a business setting. You would usually use a verb such as *climb* with this phrase to indicate that one is going *up*, rather than *down* the corporate ladder.
Example: *You are climbing the corporate ladder faster than anyone I know. What's your secret?*

Cost an arm and a leg (also, **charge** or **pay an arm and a leg**) **(Ch. 10):** to be very expensive or overpriced.
You may insert an object pronoun after *cost* or *charge.*
Example: *The concert tickets cost me an arm and a leg!*

Cough up (Ch. 10): give up something unwillingly.
The object of this phrasal verb may be inserted either after *cough* or after *up*. However, an object pronoun, such as *it* can only be placed after *cough.*
Example: *I know you have the money. Cough it up!* (**Not Cough up it.**)

Couldn't care less (Ch. 9): to not care at all.
This idiom is commonly changed by native speakers to *could care less* (*I could care less about him*); however, note that this is an *incorrect* usage of the phrase.
Example: *I couldn't care less whether we have green beans or peas with dinner. Either is fine.*

Cross that bridge when one comes to it (Ch. 3): to deal with a situation or a problem when one has to, and not before.
Example: *There's no use in worrying about what we'll do if there is a Third World War. We'll cross that bridge when we come to it.*

Cut corners (Ch. 3): to compromise on quality; to do something poorly or incompletely.
Example: *Many people have speculated that the space shuttle blew up because NASA cut corners when they tested the equipment.*

Cut it out (Ch. 9): stop it!
This idiom can be used as a command or in reported speech. Use this idiom with caution; you would use it if you were *not* concerned with being nice or tactful.
Example: *The children were dumping their food onto the floor when the teacher walked in and told them to cut it out.*

Doesn't grow on trees (Ch. 10): is not readily available or easy to obtain (frequently used when speaking of money). This idiom is always used in the negative.
Example: *I know good secretaries don't grow on trees, but I'm confident that we'll find someone to fill the position soon.*

Dressed to kill (Ch. 8): dressed in a very attractive and alluring way.
Example: *Marian was dressed to kill when she was photographed for the cover of* Vogue *magazine.*

Drive someone crazy (Ch. 9): to severely annoy or irritate someone.
Example: *Mrs. O'Neely calls me every day at five o'clock just to ask what time it is. She's driving me crazy!*

Drop in (Ch. 11): to pay someone a short, informal visit.
Drop in can be used without further explanation.
Example: *I'm glad you dropped in.*
It can also be followed by *on*.
Example: *I dropped in* <u>*on*</u> *Susie, but she was busy with a client.*

Egg on one's face (Ch. 11): to be humiliated and embarrassed by claiming something that is subsequently proved false.
Example: *Tim told everyone Jane was in love with him. He had egg on his face when she ran off with Bruce.*

Fairweather friend (Ch. 11): someone who is a friend only when you are very successful; if your success or popularity diminishes, he/she is no longer friendly.
Example: *I didn't realize how many fairweather friends I had until I lost my job.*

Fast track (Ch. 7): a faster-than-normal rise through the ranks of an organization.
You are *on* the fast track if you are promoted more often than others in the same company. (Note the preposition used with this phrase.)
Example: *Don't be discouraged if you aren't promoted this time. Not everyone can be on the fast track.*

Feather in one's cap (Ch. 4): an accomplishment of which one can be very proud.
Example: *After staying home and raising a family for seventeen years, Patricia went back to college to finish her degree. That diploma was a real feather in her cap.*

Feather one's nest (Ch. 7): to furnish your home comfortably and acquire other material possessions.
Example: *Your home is beautiful! You've done a great job feathering your nest.*
Note: This idiom is also used to refer to corrupt or unscrupulous people in positions of power who use money illegally for their own purposes.
Example: *The city councilman was using our tax dollars to feather his nest!*

Feel ten feet tall (Ch. 2): to feel happy, fortunate, and self-confident.
Example: *The applause made the actor feel ten feet tall.*

Fine line (Ch. 1): A very subtle distinction between two different things.
This idiom is usually followed by *between __ and __.*
Example: *There is a fine line between criticism and advice.*

Flash in the pan (Ch. 4): someone or something that experiences fleeting and transitory fame or popularity.
Example: *Rubik's cubes were a flash in the pan; after a short burst of popularity, they almost immediately disappeared from the market.*

Floor someone (Ch. 11): to shock or surprise someone. This idiom is often used in the passive voice.
Example: *I was floored when I won the lottery!*

Follow in someone's footsteps (Ch. 7): to follow someone's example.
Example: *Her father spent most of his life in prison; I hope she doesn't follow in his footsteps.*

For a song (Ch. 10): for very little money.
Example: *The lamp was slightly damaged, so the manager let me have it for a song.*

Four-letter words (Ch. 9): swear words; crude or crass language.
This idiom is a euphemism for language that probably should not be used in most situations. It comes from the fact that many common swear words in English have four letters.
Example: *He was really angry! I've never heard so many four-letter words!*

Get a leg up on someone (Ch. 6): get an advantage over someone.
Example: *Steve stayed home and practiced while I went out dancing, so he got a leg up on me in the competition.*

Get a rise out of someone (Ch. 9): to provoke a strong reaction of some kind.
Example: *Hoping to get a rise out of him, the police told the prisoner that if he didn't cooperate he would spend the rest of his life in prison, but he just sat quietly and stared straight ahead.*

Get something/someone off one's mind (Ch. 2): to be unable to stop thinking about someone or something; to think of something or someone constantly. This idiom is always used in the negative.
Example: *I can't get that news report off my mind. The story about the Siamese twins was fascinating.*
You may substitute *it* for *something/someone.*
Example: *I saw a fascinating new report about Siamese twins. I can't get it off my mind.*

Get one's gears turning (Ch. 12): to start thinking creatively in order to solve a problem.
Example: *You've got to plan the entire advertising campaign in the next few days, so get your gears turning.*

Get one's hands on something (Ch. 10): to obtain or acquire something.
Example: *I'm anxious to get my hands on one of those brand-new video disc players.*

This idiom is also often used as a threat, usually spoken in anger. The implication is that the speaker intends to inflict harm or punishment on another person.
Example: *Jared wrecked my car! Wait till I get my hands on him! He'll be sorry!*

Get rolling (Ch. 12): get started.
Example: *We've got about 500 miles to travel today, so we'd better get rolling.*

Get something off the ground (Ch. 3): get something started or running smoothly.
Something usually refers to a project, an idea, or a plan.
Example: *I've spent six months trying to get my new business off the ground.*

Get the picture (Ch. 11): to fully understand a situation.
This idiom stands alone; you would never say *get the picture of.* *The picture* always refers to an entire situation, never to a specific person or thing. This phrase is also often used as a nongrammatical, idiomatic question: *Get the picture?* rather than *Get the picture?* (Do you understand?)
Example: *If you ever come here again, I'll call the police. Do you get the picture?—Yeah, I got the picture.*

Give someone a break (Ch. 9): give someone a chance. (Also **get a break:** to be lucky; to be faced with a great opportunity.)
Example: *Although Jimmy didn't score very well on their placement test, the school gave him a break and let him in anyway.*

Give someone a ring (Ch. 2): to call someone on the telephone.
The placement of the object cannot vary; you cannot *give a ring to Joe,* for example; you must *give Joe a ring.*
Example: *Why don't you give me a ring when you get home?*

Give someone the runaround (or get the runaround) (Ch. 12): to be constantly referred elsewhere when one is trying to obtain something; to be given countless excuses and delays.
Example: *If there were one central office to process all requests, our customers would not get the runaround.*

Go belly-up (Ch. 12): to go bankrupt; to go out of business.
Example: *Catherine tried hard to run a bakery business out of her home, but after the new grocery store opened, she went belly-up.*

Go by the book (Ch. 12): to follow the rules; to be rigid and inflexible in fulfilling one's duties.
Example: *The new cancer drug looks very promising, but it won't be available for several years. The approval process is quite complex, and the drug companies must go by the book.*

Go to great lengths (Ch. 6): to try very, very hard.
Example: *I would go to great lengths to get this contract, but I won't do anything illegal.*

Go to the ends of the earth (Ch. 6): to do anything and everything possible.

This idiom is often used to illustrate one's dedication or devotion to someone.

Example: *Michael is so deeply in love with Jane that he would go to the ends of the earth for her.*

Hand over fist (Ch. 4): very quickly and in large amounts.

This idiom is almost always preceded by a phrase having to do with making money.

Example: *She made a fortune hand over fist by selling her collection of rare coins and stamps.*

Hands down (Ch. 4): easily, without a doubt.

Example: *Laura won the speech contest hands down. She gave the best speech I've ever heard.*

Hang on (Ch. 10): to endure a difficult situation; to persist in a particular course of action.

Do not insert anything between *hang* and *on*.

Example: *Don't give up on your piano lessons now. I know that if you hang on, it will soon get much easier.*

Have a blast (*or* be a blast) (Ch. 8): to have a lot of fun; a great time.

Example: *Thanks for inviting me to your party. I had a blast!* (**OR** *It was a blast!*)

Have a corner on something (Ch. 4): to have a monopoly on something.

Example: *Hollywood no longer has a corner on good movies. Foreign films are becoming more sophisticated and are increasingly popular.*

Something is often replaced by *the market.*

Example: *For a long time IBM had a corner on the market of personal computers.*

Have a good head on one's shoulders (Ch. 6): to be intelligent and sensible.

Example: *Since Dave came into the department, we've done things a lot more sensibly. He's got a good head on his shoulders.*

Have a nose for something (Ch. 7): to have an instinctual sense for choosing or finding something.

Be sure to say what you have a nose for; it is usually a noun.

Example: *Mr. Kramer didn't really have to work very hard to get rich; he just has a nose for money.*

Have an edge (or have *the* edge) (Ch. 6): to have an advantage over someone or something.

This idiom can be used alone (i.e., Between the two, I think Sue has the edge.)

Example: *It's hard to tell which of the cars will win the race, but I think that blue Camaro has an edge.*

It can also be followed by *on.*

Example: *Sue has an edge on Marie.*

Have it both ways (Ch. 1): To have two things at the same time that are incompatible with each other.

This idiom is usually used in the negative. Do not try to replace *it* with anything.

Example: *I'd love to have the cultural advantages of living in the city without the traffic and congestion, but I know I can't have it both ways.*

Head over heels in love (Ch. 2): very much in love.

You can be head over heels in love *with* someone, or simply head over heels in love.

Example: *Mary and Bob are head over heels in love.*

Sometimes *in love* is omitted from the expression; it is understood without being explicitly stated.

Example: *Are they really in love with each other? Oh, yes! Head over heels!*

In over one's head (Ch. 3): involved in something that is too difficult, complicated, or dangerous for one to handle easily.

You can *get* or *be* in over your head.

Example: *The drug dealers suspect that Melinda is an undercover agent, and this is her first time dealing with dangerous criminals. She's in over her head.*

In the black (Ch. 10): out of debt.

Example: *I finally paid off all my debts. I'm in the black again!*

In the red (Ch. 10): in debt, or losing money.

You can also say *go into* or *come out of* the black or the red.

Example: *I credit my stockbroker for taking me out of the red and into the black.*

Keep a level head (Ch. 3): to think calmly and rationally; to not panic.

Example: *After the accident, Marty kept a level head in spite of her injuries. She made sure everyone else was OK, and got all the necessary information from the other driver.*

Keep something bottled up (Ch. 11): to keep something secret for a period of time.

Something is often replaced by *it.*

Example: *Liz didn't want to tell anyone she had been fired from her job. She kept it bottled up for months.*

Note: This idiom is also used when one refrains from expressing strong feelings about something or when emotion is hidden from others.

Example: *I didn't cry when my father died. I kept everything bottled up.*

Keep up with the Joneses (Ch. 8): to compete with one's neighbors or associates in the accumulation of money or objects; to buy the same material goods they possess.

Example: *You don't even know how to sail! The only reason you want a boat is to keep up with the Joneses.*

Keep up with the times (Ch. 7): to be up-to-date; in touch with modern trends.

This idiom is used to reflect more than knowledge of current events; it indicates the active use of modern technology and/or theory.

Example: *It's hard to believe Mrs. Cleary is almost eighty years old. You can tell by the way she dresses and the car she drives that she keeps up with the times.*

Know where one stands (Ch. 2): to know how someone feels about you; to understand another's expectations in a relationship.

This is used in cases where the speaker is confused about the nature of his/her relationship with another person. Be sure to make *one* agree with the subject.

Example: *"I need to know where I stand with you."*

The last word (or **have the last word**) **(Ch. 11):** the final point in a discussion or argument.

This idiom may be followed by *in*.

Example: *The boss always gets the last word in hiring a new secretary.*

It can also stand alone.

Example: *I hate discussing anything with Mindy. She always has to get the last word.*

Lay it on thick (Ch. 2): to flatter or praise someone excessively.

Don't try to substitute anything else for *it* in this expression.

Example: *The movie producer kept telling her that she was the best actress he had ever seen. Boy, was he laying it on thick!*

Learn the ropes (also **to show someone the ropes** and **to know the ropes**) **(Ch. 12):** to learn how things are done or how to do something.

The in *learn the ropes* cannot be changed to a possessive adjective. *Ropes* is always plural.

Example: *It took a while to learn the ropes in my scuba diving class, but after my first dive, it was pretty easy.*

Let someone down (Ch. 6): to disappoint someone.

Example: *I expect you to be there on time. Don't let me down!*

Live it up (Ch. 8): to enjoy oneself to the fullest, without any constraints.

Do not try to substitute any other noun or pronoun for *it*.

Example: *It's your birthday! Live it up!*

Live within one's means (Ch. 10): to spend only as much money as one makes.

The possessive adjective that replaces *one's* must refer to the subject; you cannot say, for example, *You're living within my means.*

Example: *I'm sure we can live within our means if we are very careful about how we spend our money.*

Look like a million bucks (Ch. 2): to look great; to be attractive and well-dressed.

Example: *Did you see Tom Cruise in his latest movie? He looked like a million bucks in that black leather jacket!*

Make a mark (Ch. 4): to have a significant impact on something.

Example: *Even after thirty years, some of the people Sally taught in first grade still remember her. She really made a mark on her students.*

Make a plug (Ch. 1): To speak out in support of something or someone; to publicize something.

Be sure to say what you are making a plug *for*.

Example: *The owners of The Pasta Pot were at the food fair to make a plug for their new restaurant.*

Make a splash (Ch. 6): to attract a lot of attention.

Example: *The play opened in New York last week, and it really made a splash. Everyone is talking about it!*

Make mountains out of molehills (Ch. 9): to exaggerate the importance of something; to make a minor, insignificant issue into something major.

Example: *Although the doctor tried to tell her it was nothing, the young mother was distraught over her child's rash. She insisted on making mountains out of molehills.*

Make one's day (Ch. 8): to make one very happy.

Example: *I'm so glad you came to see my show. It made my day.*

Make something fly (Ch. 7): to successfully implement a plan or idea; to make it work.

Example: *Alexander Graham Bell had an idea about how people could communicate over long distances, and he made it fly. Now, almost every home has a telephone.*

Make waves (Ch. 11): to cause a commotion; to provoke attention.

Example: *George made waves when he came to dinner in women's clothes.*

Mean beans (Ch. 9): to be totally insignificant; to mean nothing.

This idiom is used both in a negative and positive form, with no change in meaning. It should be used in very informal contexts, mostly in spoken English.

Example: *This job doesn't mean beans to me.* **OR** *This job means beans to me.*

Mean business (Ch. 7): to be very serious and committed to achieving a particular objective.

In most cases, only people can mean business. This idiom usually stands alone; you would not say, for example, *He means business by the way he works.*

Example: *There's a gang of bank robbers that you should watch out for. The police have warned that they mean business.*

Middle-of-the-road (Ch. 12): average; mediocre.
Example: *The Roadside Café serves middle-of-the-road hamburgers. I think they're much better at Rosie's Kitchen.*

Miss the boat (Ch. 5): to lose a chance or opportunity to do something, often because one's response is too late or slow.
Example: *"Did you sign up for the tour of Los Angeles?" "No, I was too late. I guess I missed the boat."*

Nest egg (Ch. 7): money that is saved, especially for retirement or for when one can no longer work.
It is common to refer to the *size* of the nest egg as being small, good-sized, large, and so on. Although *nest egg* refers to savings; the verb *save* is not usually used with this phrase.
Example: *I built up my nest egg for forty years, but after the earthquake hit, I had to use it all to repair the damage to our home.*

No ifs, ands, or buts (Ch. 1): Absolutely no excuses; without any doubt, dissension, or variance.
This phrase is often followed by *about it*.
Example: *I have to be in class at seven o'clock tomorrow, no ifs, ands, or buts about it.*

No strings attached (Ch. 2): with no commitment or conditions set.
Example: *I told him I was willing to review his case with no strings attached. Neither one of us was bound to sign a contract until I finished the review.*

No sweat (Ch. 12): without any problem; easily.
Example: *"Who won the race?" "Oh, Jackie did, no sweat."*

Not have a prayer (Ch. 5): to have no chance at all.
This idiom is always used in the negative.
Example: *With his poor grades, Jason doesn't have a prayer of getting into Harvard.*

Not see the forest for the trees (Ch. 1): To be overly preoccupied with the details and unable to see a problem as a whole.
This idiom is always used in the negative form.
Example: *I was so concerned about finding the two dollars I was missing that I didn't notice that the whole house had been robbed. I couldn't see the forest for the trees.*

Odds are (Ch. 3): it is probable; the chances are good.
This idiom usually begins the sentence or phrase.
Example: *Odds are we're not going to get much sleep tonight with a party going on next door.*

Off the beaten path (Ch. 4): different, unusual, or unfamiliar.
This idiom can be used in the more literal sense to mean a place that is not well known or traveled.
Example: *We don't want to go to Hawaii on our honeymoon; we're hoping to go someplace off the beaten path.*

Or it can refer to someone's ideas or behavior.
Example: *I thought the professor's theories were interesting, although they're not widely accepted. He's a little off the beaten path.*

Off the top of one's head (Ch. 3): to think of something without looking it up or trying hard to figure it out.
Example: *Off the top of your head, can you remember the fifth president of the United States?*

On the go (Ch. 6): constantly busy.
You cannot be on the go *somewhere*; don't try to follow *go* with a place.
Example: *You'll have to schedule an appointment with Mr. Luther a week in advance. He's always on the go.*

On the house (Ch. 8): provided free of charge by the establishment.
Example: *Have a drink. It's on the house.*

Open a can of worms (Ch. 3): to create a whole new set of problems to deal with.
Example: *Every time someone reveals a new theory on John F. Kennedy's death, it opens a can of worms.*

Open doors (Ch. 7): to provide opportunities for people to get ahead in some way.
Open in this phrase is a verb, not an adjective; you must say for whom you are opening doors.
Example: *The coaches at the inner-city recreation center are opening doors for young athletes who can't afford to train at more expensive clubs.*

Out of this world (Ch. 11): fantastic, extraordinary.
Example: *This cake is out of this world! Will you give me the recipe?*

Paint the town red (Ch. 8): to go out and have a good time.
Example: *The night before he got married, Matthew went out and painted the town red.*

Promise the moon (Ch. 2): to promise someone something that is impossible.
The placement of the indirect object can be varied or omitted entirely.
> *I wish I could promise you the moon.* **OR**
> *I wish I could promise the moon to you.* **OR**
> *I wish I could promise the moon.*

Pros and cons (Ch. 1): The advantages and disadvantages.
Example: *I'm planning to buy a new car. Do you know the pros and cons of this model?*

Put one's best foot forward (Ch. 6): to try one's best; to try to make a good impression.
Example: *Cynthia was determined to impress her guests at the dinner party. She put her best foot forward.*

Put one's name on the line (Ch. 4): to risk losing one's reputation (or whatever it is that has been put on the line.)
Example: *I'm willing to put my name on the line to support the new candidate for mayor.*
Instead of *name*, you can also say *reputation, job, life, money,* and the like.
Example: *Charles put his life on the line to rescue the dog from the burning house.*

Put someone on a pedestal (Ch. 2): to be in awe of someone; to believe that he/she can do no wrong.
This expression may be used in the passive voice.
Example: *Elvis Presley was put on a pedestal throughout his career, so it was a shock to his fans when he died of a drug overdose.*

Raise eyebrows (Ch. 4): to cause disapproval, or mild shock.
This idiom is often expressed as *raise some eyebrows*, or *raise a few eyebrows*.
Example: *I'm sure Caroline raised some eyebrows when she refused to reveal who the father of her child was.*

Right around the corner (or **just around the corner**) **(Ch. 3):** imminent; about to happen; in the near future.
Example: *I'm sure that cars will soon be obsolete. A more efficient mode of transportation is right around the corner.*

Right under one's nose (Ch. 1): In plain view; in a place where something or someone might be easily noticed.
Example: *Bobby ate one of the freshly baked cookies right under his mother's nose.*

Rule out (Ch. 1): Eliminate something.
The object can be placed either after *rule* or after *out*; however, if the object is a pronoun, it must go after *rule*.
Examples: *That movie was nominated for an Academy Award. However, the Director's Guild didn't like it, and so they ruled it out. (**NOT** They ruled out it.)*
OR *The Director's Guild ruled out that movie for an Academy Award.*
This idiom is also commonly used in the passive voice.
Example: *Any chances for that movie to win the Academy Award have been ruled out.*

Save face (Ch. 5): to preserve one's good reputation or dignity after doing something that may potentially damage that reputation.
Example: *After the scandal that had erupted in the police department, it was impossible for the chief of police to save face.*

Contrast **lose face:** to lose one's dignity or ruin one's good reputation.
Save face and *lose face* are used without any possessive adjective; you would never say, for example, *He saved his face,* or *I lost my face.*

Example: *The president of the company lost face with his employees when he was accused of cheating on his tax return.*

Search high and low (Ch. 10): to look everywhere for something.
Example: *I've searched high and low for our passports, but I can't find them.*

See something in a whole new light (or **put something in a new light**) **(Ch. 1):** To view or understand something from a different perspective.
Example: *You didn't tell me they offered twice as much money to buy the jewels. That puts their offer in a whole new light!*

Show one's true colors (Ch. 9): to reveal one's true character; to show what one is really like.
Example: *Mrs. Mayfair says she is not racist, but she showed her true colors when she refused to hire Stan Kim just because he's Asian.*

Sitting duck (Ch. 5): someone in a vulnerable or unguarded position who is unaware of the danger of the situation.
Example: *Tourists who carry a lot of cash on them are sitting ducks for the gangs of pickpockets that roam the streets.*

Slip one's mind (Ch. 3): to briefly forget something that one was supposed to remember.
The thing that is forgotten is always the subject of the phrase: *I forgot the appointment: The appointment slipped my mind.*
Example: *I was going to pick up the clothes from the cleaners, but it slipped my mind.*

Slip through one's fingers (Ch. 5): to be lost or to narrowly escape without one knowing how.
This idiom implies that one is very close to succeeding when the objective is somehow lost.
Example: *Hank went fishing yesterday, but he only caught a couple of tiny trout. He says the big ones always slip through his fingers.*

Snowed under (Ch. 12): to be overwhelmed by too much work.
Example: *The government lawyers can't possibly handle all the cases they have; they're snowed under!*
This idiom may also be used to describe a situation in which someone gets too much of something to be able to respond adequately.
Example: *When Mrs. Ho was appointed to the committee, she was snowed under by congratulatory cards and phone calls.*

Stack up (Ch. 12): to compare with something similar.
Example: *I wonder how the quality of man-made diamonds stacks up against that of natural diamonds.*
You can say that something stacks up *against* or *to* the thing with which you are comparing it. It can also be used alone to say that something compares favorably with its competitors.
Example: *Macintosh computers really stack up.*

Stars in one's eyes (Ch. 2): to have feelings of great happiness and excitement (usually caused by being in love).
Example: *Teresa smiled at Sam after class today, and he walked around all afternoon with stars in his eyes.*
This idiom is also sometimes used to describe someone who is obsessed with show business.
Example: *I've always wanted to be an actress. I guess you could say I've got stars in my eyes.*

Stay in touch (Ch. 11): to maintain contact with friends and acquaintances.
This idiom can stand alone, or it can be followed by *with*.
Example: *Even though we live in different cities, we've stayed in touch with each other for more than ten years.*

Stay put (Ch. 10): to stay in one place; to not move.
Stay and *put* cannot be separated.
Example: *You should not expect your three-year-old child to stay put for very long.*

Stick one's neck out (Ch. 6): to take a risk.
Example: *You really stuck your neck out to defend me against that mob. They could have killed you!*

Stop something (or someone) in its tracks (Ch. 5): to stop something or someone very abruptly or forcefully.
Example: *When we moved into our new house there were millions of cockroaches, but we stopped them in their tracks with a strong insecticide.*

Stretched too thin (also to spread oneself too thin) (Ch. 10): to have so many expenses that one cannot pay them all; or to be involved in so many activities that one cannot do any of them well.
A person is usually what is stretched too thin, but money can be as well. Do not try to change the form of *stretched*.
Example: *I can't help on the committee this year; I'm already stretched too thin.*

Strike a chord (Ch. 4): to seem familiar; to be in agreement with one's ideas or feelings.
Example: *Columbus's theory that the world was not flat struck a chord with a few other scientists of his day; there were others who also believed the world was round.*

Take a hike (Ch. 9): go away!
Be careful when using this idiom; it implies anger and probably should *not* be used with an authority figure. This idiom can be used either as a command or reported speech.
Example: *I never want to see you again. Take a hike!*

Take center stage (Ch. 4): to be the center of attention.
Example: *The bride should always take center stage at her own wedding.*

Take it easy (Ch. 8): to relax and not worry about anything.
Example: *I'm sure you'll be fine when you make your first parachute jump. Just take it easy.*

Take it out on someone (Ch. 5): to act in a mean, angry, or hostile way toward someone, even if it is not that person's fault that you are angry.
Example: *Trina was angry that the kids broke a window while they were playing baseball, and she took it out on her husband when he got home.*
The actual emotion one is expressing can be used in place of *it*.
Example: *The nurse took her frustrations out on her patients.*

Take one's breath away (Ch. 8): to impress greatly or to amaze with the beauty or wonder of something.
Example: *Have you ever been to Niagara Falls? It will take your breath away!*

Take someone to the cleaners (Ch. 10): to overcharge or to cheat someone willfully out of his/her money.
Only people can be the subject of this phrase.
Example: *It has been suggested that many auto mechanics will take their female customers to the cleaners because women aren't generally well-informed about their cars.*

Take something in stride (Ch. 6): to accept a difficult situation and move on.
The word or phrase that replaces *something* may come after *take* or after *in stride*.
Example: *He took in stride the death of his young wife, and kept working as she would have wanted him to.*

Take the heat (Ch. 7): to handle the pressure in a difficult situation; to be held responsible for problems or mistakes.
The cannot be replaced by a possessive adjective; you can *take the heat*, but you cannot *take your heat*.
Example: *I'm thinking about making Rita my public relations manager. Do you think she can take the heat?*

Throw in the towel (Ch. 3): to quit; give up.
Example: *After dancing on Broadway for twelve years, she finally threw in the towel.*

Till the cows come home (Ch. 3): for a very, very long time.
Example: *Are you just going to read your book till the cows come home?*

To the letter (Ch. 12): exactly as something is supposed to be done, without variation or flexibility.
Example: *We followed the treasure map to the letter, but there was nothing there.*

Toe the line (Ch. 6): to do exactly what is expected; to follow orders.
Example: *Your behavior is unacceptable. You're going to have to toe the line or suffer the consequences.*

Too close for comfort (Ch. 5): dangerously close.
Example: *The speeding train nearly hit us. That was too close for comfort!*

Top banana (Ch. 7): the head of an organization; the person in charge; the leader.
This term can only be used with the definite article (*the*); you cannot use a possessive adjective as you might with *my boss*.
Example: *The President is the top banana in the United States government.*

Top-of-the-line (Ch. 8): of the highest quality.
Example: *The Stealth Fighter is the military's top-of-the-line jet.*

Travel in the wrong circles (Ch. 11): to associate with the wrong people.
Example: *I'm not at all pleased with my daughter's new friends. I think she's traveling in the wrong circles.*

Up in the air (Ch. 1): Uncertain; unknown; undecided.
Concrete nouns are not usually used as the subject of this phrase; issues, ideas, questions, or problems are more likely to be *up in the air*. You can paraphrase these as *things*, or *it*.

Example: *After her horrible accident, the doctors don't know if she will live or die. It's still up in the air.*

Uphill battle (Ch. 5): a very difficult task.
Example: *Trying to keep children from getting dirty is an uphill battle.*

Warm up to (Ch. 4): to accept and come to like something that one at first does not like.
Example: *I know you were not impressed with Renae when you first met her, but I'm sure in time you'll warm up to her.*

Wipe out (Ch. 5): to destroy; eliminate.
Example: *The army wiped out their enemies' arsenal of weapons in one strategic attack.*
The object can either go between *wipe* and *out* or after *wipe out*.
Example: *Researchers are trying to wipe cancer out,* **OR** *Researchers are trying to wipe out cancer.*

Worth one's salt (Ch. 12): to be worth one's paid salary.
Example: *Barry is a terrible salesman. He's definitely not worth his salt.*

TAPESCRIPT AND ANSWER KEY

CHAPTER 1 NEGOTIATION

TAPESCRIPT

D. Choosing the Best Answer
1. The actress appeared on several news and talk shows to talk about her new movie.
2. If you're planning on getting married, you will have to stop going out with other women.
3. The students are angry over the school's new pass/fail policy. They feel their efforts should be rewarded with a wider range of marks.
4. Lisa was the best secretary Mr. Thomas ever had, but he suddenly fired her because he thought her hairdo made her look unprofessional.
5. I can't believe the thieves stole the painting with the museum guard so nearby!
6. Susie's outfits are always so daring and different. I can't decide if she has a great sense of style or no fashion sense at all.
7. We need someone who has previous managerial experience for this job, and George has never been a manager.
8. Sharon refuses to negotiate the terms of her contract. She will not compromise.
9. I thought it would be easy to be a mother, but now that I have a child, my opinion has changed considerably.
10. Doctors are split on the issue of nationalized health care; they are quick to take sides and debate the points of different health care plans.
11. Nancy thought Greg was selfish and vain. However, it wasn't long before they were seeing each other regularly.
12. The score is five to five with seven minutes left in the game.

ANSWER KEY

D. Choosing the Best Answer

1. b	5. b	9. c
2. a	6. c	10. c
3. a	7. a	11. b
4. a	8. c	12. c

E. Retelling the Story
These answers are provided as examples only; other answers are possible.
1. Not all cases that are tried in a court of law are black and white.
2. It is sometimes difficult to determine who is at fault in a case; there is a fine line between innocence and guilt.
3. The men killed their dog right under their neighbor's nose, and the neighbor then called the police.
4. Animal rights activists used the publicity of the trial to make a plug for their organization.
5. Those who condemned the men's actions said that they should be punished severely; no ifs, ands, or buts about it.
6. Others, who did not think the men were criminals, said that the activists could not see the forest for the trees.
7. They said that if some of the self-righteous Americans would consider the case carefully, they might see things in a whole new light.
8. The experience of living abroad might make many Americans change their tune completely.

9. The defense attorney argued that the men hadn't known what they had done was wrong, so any thought that they broke the law intentionally must be ruled out.
10. The prosecutor said the men could not have it both ways.
11. The verdict in the trial was up in the air.
12. The jury argued the pros and cons of each side in the case.

F. Putting the Idioms into Practice
Part I
These answers are provided as examples only; other answers are possible.
Scott Darby believes the government can take care of education best, no ifs, ands, or buts about it. . . . He changed his tune on health care after some doctors contributed to his campaign. . . .
Francine Lewis wants to have it both ways . . . . She would like to discuss the pros and cons of private education before deciding. . . . She often makes a plug for health care workers. . . .
Part II
1. black and white
2. right under the nose
3. fine line
4. see things in a whole new light
5. can't see the forest for the trees
6. up in the air

CHAPTER 2 ROMANCE

TAPESCRIPT

D. Choosing the Best Answer
1. She's a married woman, but Doug is head over heels in love.
2. After going out with Ken, Marty had stars in her eyes.
3. I heard that song again on the radio, and now I can't get it off my mind.
4. Dressed in his white uniform, Sergeant Gibbs looks like a million bucks.
5. Charlotte was just crowned Miss America. She must feel ten feet tall!
6. Kurt's girlfriend hasn't seen him for weeks, and she doesn't know where she stands.
7. Although Dr. Carter's experiments in cancer research look very hopeful, she knows that she can't promise the moon.
8. It's time we recognize that police officers make mistakes just like everyone else; it's not fair to put them on a pedestal.
9. When Stewart met his future mother-in-law, he really laid it on thick.
10. Lena feels that her parents don't give her any breathing room.
11. You may test drive this car with no strings attached.
12. Darryl had some questions about the wedding plans, so he gave Christine a ring.

ANSWER KEY

D. Choosing the Best Answer

1. F	5. F	9. F
2. T	6. F	10. T
3. T	7. T	11. F
4. F	8. T	12. F

E. Retelling the Story
These answers are provided as examples only; other answers are possible.
1. John was head over heels in love with Tina, even though they had only just met.
2. From the moment he saw her, John had stars in his eyes.

3. He couldn't get her off his mind.
4. Tina looked like a million bucks!
5. Tina made John feel ten feet tall when he was with her.
6. John wanted to know where he stood with Tina.
7. He knew he couldn't promise her the moon, but he would do his best.
8. Tina felt that John had put her on a pedestal.
9. Tina thought that John had spent the evening laying it on thick.
10. Tina wanted to be independent. She needed some breathing room.
11. She wanted a casual relationship, with no strings attached.
12. Tina wanted Lori to give her a ring.

F. Putting the Idioms into Practice
These answers are provided as examples only; other answers are possible.
1. I don't know where I stand.
2. You always look like a million bucks.
3. Quit laying it on thick.
4. I need some breathing room.
5. I can't get you off my mind.
6. You have put me on a pedestal.
7. I feel ten feet tall.
8. You had stars in your eyes.
9. We were head over heels in love.
10. We can see each other with no strings attached.
11. I can't promise you the moon.
12. Please give me a ring.

CHAPTER 3 PROBLEM SOLVING

TAPESCRIPT

D. Choosing the Best Answer
1. Our anniversary better not slip your mind again!
2. If Jenny doesn't blow her next dive, she should win the medal.
3. Calvin can change a flat tire, but if anything is wrong with the engine, he's in over his head.
4. In 1900, the world did not realize that air travel was just around the corner.
5. Our shelter for the homeless is projected to open in two months, but we need a lot of volunteers to get it off the ground.
6. Odds are the president won't be reelected.
7. You can't cut corners when you're making bread.
8. We had been walking around Boston for hours when we realized we were lost. Gina was the only one who kept a level head.
9. I could study till the cows come home, and it still wouldn't make any difference.
10. If you ask Cindy about her ex-husband, you'll open a can of worms.
11. After four women turned Louis down, he decided to throw in the towel.
12. Don't worry about what to do when your grandfather is gone. You can cross that bridge when you come to it.
13. No matter how many numbers you give her to add, Sabrina can tell you the total off the top of her head!

ANSWER KEY

D. Choosing the Best Answer
1. a	6. b	10. b
2. b	7. a	11. a
3. b	8. a	12. b
4. a	9. a	13. b
5. b		

E. Retelling the Story
These answers are provided as examples only; other answers are possible.
1. When Bernie asks Alfred if he has called Dr. Bleeb, Alfred replies that it slipped his mind.
2. Bernie is worried that Alfred will blow his chances of seeing Betsy again.
3. Alfred believes he is in over his head.
4. Bernie thinks that success in this project is right around the corner.
5. If they want to save Betsy, they have to get their time travel machine off the ground.
6. Odds are that it is impossible.
7. Alfred can't cut corners; each experiment has to be conducted thoroughly.
8. Bernie needs to keep a level head.
9. It is possible that Alfred might work on the project till the cows come home and still not know how to solve the problem.
10. Each time he tries something new, Alfred opens a can of worms.
11. Bernie does not want Alfred to throw in the towel.
12. It is possible that they may fail to rescue Betsy, but they will cross that bridge when they come to it.
13. Bernie asks Alfred if he knows off the top of his head what would happen if he put two wires together.

F. Putting the Idioms into Practice
1. get off the ground
2. right around the corner
3. in over their heads
4. blew it
5. opened a can of worms
6. Odds are
7. It probably slipped their minds
8. keep a level head
9. cut corners
10. off the top of your head
11. till the cows come home
12. throw in the towel
13. cross that bridge when we come to it

CHAPTER 4 MAKING AN IMPRESSION

TAPESCRIPT

D. Choosing the Best Answer
1. Henry Ford, a pioneer in the automobile industry, was ahead of his time.
2. I thought James would be making money hand over fist by now, but instead he's going broke.
3. The Republicans usually have a corner on the vote in Utah.
4. Anna Billings put her life on the line when she confronted the angry mob.
5. The government wasn't willing to provide the remote settlement with food and other supplies because it was too far off the beaten path.
6. Although the actress had won many awards before, being nominated for the Oscar was a real feather in her cap.
7. Although they were only here for a few months, the Fishers certainly made a mark on this community.
8. Predictably, the senator's proposal to legalize drugs raised some eyebrows in Congress.
9. I know you don't think scuba diving sounds like fun, but once you try it in the Caribbean, I'm sure you'll warm up to the idea.
10. Rachel is an artist, so your discussion about the new exhibition at the museum struck a chord with her.

11. Don't challenge Teresa to a game of chess. She'll beat you hands down.
12. Bell-bottoms, miniskirts, and platform shoes were very popular in the 1960s, but like most fashion trends, they were simply a flash in the pan.
13. Eddie is a typical six-year-old. Wherever he is, he takes center stage.
14. The candidate brought the audience to its feet several times during his speech.

ANSWER KEY

D. Choosing the Best Answer

1. a	6. b	11. a
2. b	7. b	12. b
3. a	8. a	13. a
4. a	9. a	14. b
5. b	10. b	

E. Retelling the Story

These answers are provided as examples only; other answers are possible.

1. Walt Disney was ahead of his time in the movie industry.
2. Not long after he established his own production company, Walt Disney was making money hand over fist on animated films.
3. Soon he had a corner on the market of animated films.
4. Disney borrowed a lot of money and put his name on the line to build Disneyland.
5. Many people thought he was off the beaten path when he built Disneyland, but the park's success silenced his critics.
6. The addition of Disneyworld proved to be a feather in his cap.
7. Even after his death, Walt Disney continues to make a mark on the world of entertainment.
8. Mickey Mouse probably raised some eyebrows in the beginning.
9. Soon audiences began to warm up to him.
10. He struck a chord especially with children.
11. He could beat any other celebrity in a popularity contest hands down.
12. His lasting fame proves that Mickey Mouse was not just a flash in the pan.
13. Everywhere he goes, Mickey Mouse takes center stage.
14. He often brings audiences to their feet.

F. Putting the Idioms into Practice

1. raised some eyebrows/ Lady Godiva
2. have a corner on/ Michael Jackson
3. made a mark/ Rudolph Valentino
4. hands down/ Babe Ruth
5. hand over fist/ Alfred Bernhard Nobel
6. off the beaten path/ Lieutenant Hiroo Onoda
7. strike a chord/ Jim Henson
8. put his reputation on the line/ Henry Ford II
9. bring audiences to their feet/ Elvis Presley
10. ahead of his time/ Marco Polo
11. flash in the pan/ Elizabeth Taylor
12. took center stage/ Charles A. Lindbergh Jr.
13. warmed up to/ Vincent van Gogh
14. feather in her cap/ Cleopatra VII

CHAPTER 5 FACING DEFEAT

TAPESCRIPT

D. Choosing the Best Answer

1. The fire wiped out the main wing of the library, so we'll have to use other resources to get the information we need.

2. The last contestant really missed the boat on that game show.
3. Although the meteor landed over 200 miles away, people living in Las Vegas said it was too close for comfort.
4. The soldiers on the front lines in World War II were sitting ducks.
5. Medical researchers predict that by the year 2000 they will stop the spread of AIDS in its tracks.
6. Perhaps the United States soccer team can be truly competitive in world competition, but it will be an uphill battle.
7. There were reports that the Loch Ness Monster had been caught in a marine biologist's underwater trap, but it somehow slipped through his fingers.
8. If the world's oil supply were cut off, it would bring most of the industrialized nations to their knees.
9. Sonya is trying to learn all of Mahler's Second Symphony in one month. She has probably bitten off more than she can chew.
10. It's too bad Hank lost the account, but he really shouldn't take it out on his secretary.
11. The Gulf War proved that no single army would have a prayer against the combined military strength of the United Nations.
12. After boasting that he could pin anyone in thirty seconds, the wrestler tried to save face by claiming that he lost the match only because he had been sick.

ANSWER KEY

D. Choosing the Best Answer

1. F	5. F	9. T
2. F	6. F	10. F
3. T	7. T	11. T
4. F	8. F	12. T

E. Retelling the Story

These answers are provided as examples only; other answers are possible.

1. During a tragic period of history, the American Indians were almost wiped out.
2. The government offered the settlers free land, and many rushed to take it, not wanting to miss the boat.
3. The settlers said the Indians were too close for comfort, although the settlers had moved onto Indian land.
4. The Indians who did not cooperate with the government's plan were sitting ducks.
5. A few Indians tried to stop the settlers in their tracks, but it was a very difficult task.
6. The Indians tried to defend themselves against the settlers, but it was an uphill battle.
7. The small number of Indians who slipped through the militia's fingers were caught.
8. Lieutenant Colonel Custer wanted to bring the Indians to their knees.
9. The officer and his men realized too late that they had bitten off more than they could chew.
10. The settlers' hostility increased, and they took it out on innocent Indian women and children.
11. The unarmed Indians at Wounded Knee didn't have a prayer.
12. Many years later, the American government tried to save face by giving back some of the Indian land they had taken and paying for some land they could not give back.

F. Putting the Idioms into Practice

1. wipe out
2. miss the boat
3. save face
4. doesn't have a prayer

5. sitting ducks
6. too close for comfort
7. take it out on
8. brought the community to its knees
9. bitten off more than they can chew
10. uphill battle
11. stop the disease in its tracks
12. slip through our fingers

CHAPTER 6 EFFORT

TAPESCRIPT

D. Choosing the Best Answer

1. Although the polls show both candidates running pretty evenly, I think Senator Curtis will have the edge at the time of the election.
2. My first day on the job was a disaster—I spilled ink all over my boss's desk, and I accidentally hung up the phone on several customers. The next day I was determined to put my best foot forward.
3. We were so surprised at Shelly's behavior. How could she let us down like that?
4. Phyllis decided to give Bob another chance, but she told him he'd better toe the line or else start to look for another job.
5. Jim is such a nice man—and he's got a good head on his shoulders, too.
6. While everyone around him was hysterical over the earthquake, Joey took it in stride.
7. I'm sorry, James. I guess Billy got a leg up on you—he asked me out first. Maybe next time.
8. I know I'm sticking my neck out, but I'm going to tell Calvin that if he isn't willing to marry me, he'll have to move out. Nine years is long enough to decide!
9. Wow! You look terrific in that suit! You will certainly make a splash at the party tonight.
10. I had to bend over backwards to get the project completed on time, but it didn't make any difference.
11. Ellen, why don't you take a break? You've been on the go since six o'clock this morning.
12. Professor Wormbog is convinced that there are space aliens that regularly visit our planet, and he will go to the ends of the earth to prove his theory.
13. Roland went to great lengths to get the job, but it was worth it!

ANSWER KEY

D. Choosing the Best Answer

1. a	6. b	10. a
2. b	7. a	11. b
3. a	8. a	12. b
4. b	9. b	13. a
5. b		

E. Retelling the Story

These answers are provided as examples only; other answers are possible.

1. Do you have an edge on the people you work with?
2. If you are sick on the day of an important presentation, you should put your best foot forward anyway.
3. Or perhaps you should call in sick and tell the president you are sorry to let him down.
4. When an employee doesn't do what she is supposed to, tell her to toe the line or she will be fired.

5. Some people just don't have a good head on their shoulders.
6. If someone receives a promotion that you were hoping to get, you should take it in stride.
7. Should you tell your co-worker that you are happy that he or she got the leg up on you?
8. If your ad agency is trying to promote business, you should stick your neck out and offer your services free of charge if you do not improve a company's sales.
9. Some people might do anything to make a splash, even dress up in outrageous costumes.
10. If you are tired, but you still have work to do, you should bend over backwards to finish your work before you relax.
11. Or you might consider telling your boss that you've been on the go and you need some help to finish the project.
12. Your boss might think that you would go to the ends of the earth to help the business, but your sleep is more important.
13. If you most often chose the letter *a*, you are willing to go to great lengths to succeed.

F. Putting the Idioms into Practice

1. have a good head on your shoulders
2. get a leg up on
3. go to great lengths
4. put your best foot forward
5. make a splash with
6. toe the line
7. go to great lengths
8. stick your neck out
9. go to the ends of the earth
10. take it in stride
11. have an edge
12. let us down
13. on the go

CHAPTER 7 AMBITION

TAPESCRIPT

D. Choosing the Best Answer

1. I don't want to talk to a secretary about this problem. Who's the top banana around here?
2. The president takes the heat for everything that's wrong with this country.
3. There are a lot of problems with the proposed school lunch program. If they can't make it fly, many children will go hungry.
4. Joe doesn't ever want to be on the corporate ladder. He's content being a truck driver.
5. Take your boss to lunch. That should help if you want to get on the fast track.
6. Bruce has made millions from his collection. He has a nose for rare coins.
7. Maria is opening doors for a lot of minorities with her job placement service.
8. Mr. and Mrs. Garner are always arguing. I guess they can't agree on who calls the shots.
9. A popular ice cream company recently lost a lot of customers because they didn't keep up with the times. They were still selling only ice cream when more and more people wanted frozen yogurt.
10. Jared has dated plenty of other women, but this time he means business.
11. It would be easier to feather my nest on a salary like yours.

12. Mrs. O'Connor put her entire nest egg into the gold mine. She lost everything!

13. Although Joey admired his big brother immensely, he decided not to follow in his footsteps.

ANSWER KEY

D. Choosing the Best Answer

1. T	6. F	10. T
2. F	7. F	11. T
3. F	8. T	12. F
4. T	9. T	13. F
5. T		

E. Retelling the Story

These answers are provided as examples only; other answers are possible.

1. Cheryl Dobbs is the top banana at Astrotech Industries.
2. Although everything seems fine right now, when problems arise, Ms. Dobbs will have to take the heat.
3. There are some new projects at Astrotech, and Ms. Dobbs has to make them fly.
4. Being a woman was an advantage as well as a disadvantage to Ms. Dobbs as she climbed the corporate ladder.
5. In the beginning, she was not on the fast track.
6. However, soon Ms. Dobbs was noticed because she had a nose for good deals.
7. Her increased visibility has opened doors for other women.
8. Now that she is calling the shots, Ms. Dobbs is planning some changes at Astrotech.
9. She knows that the company must keep up with the times.
10. She also recognizes that when many women enter the workplace, they mean business.
11. A lot of women must feather their own nest.
12. Women are also very interested in building up a large nest egg for their retirement.
13. It is likely that many people will want to follow in Ms. Dobbs's footsteps.

F. Putting the Idioms into Practice

These answers are provided as examples only; other answers are possible.

1. Pablo Mayorga was the top banana at Hollyville Entertainment.
2. Although both sons took part in the murder, Joe will probably take the heat since he is the older of the two.
3. Others in the industry respected him immensely because they knew he meant business.
4. Mr. Mayorga was clearly on the fast track at Tower Pictures, and he quickly worked his way up the corporate ladder.
5. Because Pablo Mayorga wanted to call the shots, he established Hollyville Entertainment.
6. Mr. Mayorga took projects that no one else wanted, and to the surprise of his competitors, he made them fly.
7. Although he was a demanding employer, he opened a lot of doors for minorities in his company.
8. He put a lot of his profits back into the business so he could keep up with the times.
9. Pablo Mayorga was known for having a nose for popular movies.
10. The Mayorga family had a luxurious home, as Mr. Mayorga's wealth allowed him to spend a lot of money to feather his nest.
11. Mr. Mayorga wanted his sons to follow in his footsteps, but the sons wanted to go their own way.
12. The two young men were hoping to inherit their parents' nest egg after the murder.

CHAPTER 8 LEISURE

TAPESCRIPT

D. Choosing the Best Answer

1. I saw a beautiful porcelain doll in that antique store that would be perfect for my collection.
2. I've got a fifty-dollar bet on this basketball game. I would be very happy if the Lakers won.
3. The Whitmans went to Europe last summer, and now they're vacationing in Greece.
4. It was so hot outside, the kids played in the pool all afternoon.
5. Pete has a brand new stereo with more buttons and dials than you could count.
6. The bars and clubs around here don't close until around two in the morning.
7. The research library has all the information you'll need. Just ask the librarian.
8. I was amazed the first time I saw the northern lights above the Arctic Circle.
9. This restaurant doesn't charge for dessert.
10. I didn't do much over the holiday.
11. Wow! Did you see Cindy McAllister at the party last night?
12. Tony left his new boat out in front of his house for a few days just so everyone would see it.
13. Jeanine has a master's degree in engineering, so she would never consider working as a waitress, even though she needs the money.

ANSWER KEY

D. Choosing the Best Answer

1. b	6. a	10. a
2. c	7. c	11. b
3. c	8. c	12. b
4. a	9. b	13. a
5. b		

E. Retelling the Story

These answers are provided as examples only; other answers are possible.

1. Have you had enough of headaches, bills, and keeping up with the Joneses?
2. Shouldn't you take it easy?
3. Imagine a place that will take your breath away.
4. We can offer you all the benefits of a top-of-the-line resort.
5. All the comforts of the Laguna de Oro resort are right at your feet.
6. *Global Visions* said that if ordinary hotels are beneath you, you should try the Laguna de Oro.
7. Everyone at the resort will try to make your day.
8. Two of the guests of the resort wrote to say that they had a blast.
9. Another man said he had met a woman who was dressed to kill.
10. The woman immediately caught his eye.
11. One night, the couple went out together and painted the town red.
12. Another guest told all her friends that if they really wanted to live it up, they should visit the resort.
13. If you stay one week at the Laguna de Oro, your last night is on the house!

F. Putting the Idioms into Practice

These answers are provided as examples only; other answers are possible.

9:04 There are a number of attractions right at your feet, such as skiing, boating, horseback riding, hiking, and a variety of museums, art galleries, and cultural events.

9:36 I would recommend that you go to The King's Feast—it serves top-of-the-line food.

10:15 Tell him to take it easy! No earthquakes have hit Mountaincrest in over more than 300 years.

10:20 You should go see the waterfall nearby. It will take your breath away!

11:30 Take them to the zoo! They'll have a blast!

11:51 Thanks so much for calling! That makes my day!

12:12 There are several stores downtown with specialty items that may catch your eye.

2:10 The theater is quite formal, so go dressed to kill.

2:37 Your wife is just trying to keep up with the Joneses. Anyway, Mountaincrest rated higher than Atlantic City in *Tour Magazine*.

2:42 There are plenty of restaurants, bars, and night clubs to choose from. Go out and paint the town red!

2:59 Reserve a suite at the best hotel, eat at the finest restaurants in town, and live it up! You can't go wrong!

3:48 Your best option is the Mountaincrest Lodge; anything else would be beneath him.

4:10 The usual price is $200 a night, but if you pay for three nights, the fourth is on the house!

CHAPTER 9 ARGUING

TAPESCRIPT

D. Choosing the Best Answer

1. You know how much I wanted that job! I can't believe you told the boss I was irresponsible because I missed one assignment. You know I was in the hospital then!
2. Did you see Brad dumping his trash into the lake? I thought he really cared about the environment.
3. You don't have to yell at me because I forgot to buy milk at the store. It was just a little mistake!
4. I promise I won't ever cheat on a test again. Please let me have another chance!
5. You haven't spoken to me all evening. If I've done something to make you mad, please tell me.
6. Jerry's ex-wife just got married again. She was very anxious to show Jerry how handsome and rich her new husband is, but Jerry is completely uninterested in her new life.
7. I took this job because I thought I could make a difference, not because of the salary. You should know by now that the money isn't important.
8. Cliff told Jill he was going to leave her for another woman, but I don't think he would ever do it.
9. Don, I never want you to come to my office again. You're not welcome here!
10. Greg practices his drums at 3:00 in the morning when he gets home from the nightclub. It keeps me awake all night!
11. You need to learn to control yourself when you get angry. Especially when you're in the office, you must always be careful what you say to people.
12. Maryann always tries to talk to me when I'm in the middle of another project. I couldn't get any work done today because she kept interrupting me to tell me about her new boyfriend.

ANSWER KEY

D. Choosing the Best Answer

1. a	5. a	9. c
2. c	6. b	10. b
3. c	7. a	11. c
4. b	8. a	12. a

E. Retelling the Story

These answers are provided as examples only; other answers are possible.

1. Danny wanted to clear the air.
2. He thought Sara was making mountains out of molehills.
3. Danny claimed that his secretary didn't mean beans to him.
4. He said that he couldn't care less for her.
5. Sara said that Danny was showing his true colors.
6. She told him to take a hike.
7. Danny begged her to give him a break.
8. Sara said it was a cheap shot when Danny brought up a situation with her old boyfriend.
9. Danny told Sara to cut it out.
10. He said that using four-letter words wouldn't help.
11. Danny said that his secretary had been driving him crazy because she was so upset that she and her boyfriend had broken up.
12. The secretary thought she could get a rise out of Mr. Galvin if he saw her with another man.

F. Putting the Idioms into Practice

1. He's showing his true colors!
2. That's a cheap shot!
3. She's making mountains out of molehills!
4. Give him a break!
5. It's time to clear the air!
6. He obviously couldn't care less!
7. Money means beans to him!
8. He wants to get a rise out of them!
9. Tell him to take a hike!
10. Tell them to cut it out!
11. Four-letter words are inappropriate!
12. She's driving him crazy!

CHAPTER 10 MONEY

TAPESCRIPT

D. Choosing the Best Answer

1. I had to search high and low for the right gift for my mother-in-law.
2. I hoped that Ellen would learn to live within her means, but she just keeps adding to her debt.
3. I saw the same sofa advertised somewhere else for hundreds of dollars more than I paid. I saved an arm and a leg!
4. Did you hear the news? Gordon got his hands on an original Picasso!
5. I would have fixed the heater sooner, but I had to cough up the rent before the end of the month.
6. If you don't keep a record of the amount of your checks, one of them will eventually bounce.
7. Jeffrey's mother doesn't want him to try out for the school play. She's concerned that he will be stretched too thin.
8. Melissa is taking an advanced chemistry class at the university. It's a challenge, but she's hanging on.
9. In eight months Sara hasn't been out with anyone she likes. She says that nice men just don't grow on trees.

10. Mr. Burr says that he is finally ready to stay put.
11. I had my car repaired last week, and they took me to the cleaners.
12. If you wait until the peak tourist season ends, you can usually buy an airline ticket for a song.
13. This company has been operating in the red for months.
14. I paid off all my credit cards, so I'm in the black now.

ANSWER KEY

D. Choosing the Best Answer

1. F	6. F	11. F
2. F	7. T	12. F
3. T	8. T	13. F
4. F	9. F	14. T
5. T	10. T	

E. Retelling the Story

These answers are provided as examples only; other answers are possible.

1. Harry searched high and low for an apartment, but he wasn't able to find one.
2. He thinks it will be very hard to live within his means.
3. Everything costs an arm and a leg.
4. Harry tried to get his hands on a car, but he couldn't.
5. The seller of the car told Harry to cough up $500 before he would let him see it.
6. Harry bounced a check.
7. Harry is stretched too thin.
8. Harry says he will try to hang on until he finds a job.
9. Everyone knows that money doesn't grow on trees.
10. Harry is finally ready to stay put.
11. When he was looking for an apartment, a man tried to take Harry to the cleaners.
12. Joe is letting Harry live in his basement for a song.
13. As soon as he starts to work, Harry will be in the black.
14. Harry is tired of being in the red.

F. Putting the Idioms into Practice

1. stay put
2. cough up
3. stretched too thin
4. living within your means
5. costs an arm and a leg
6. for a song
7. get your hands on
8. go in the red
9. take you to the cleaners
10. search high and low
11. don't grow on trees
12. hang on
13. bounce a check
14. in the black

CHAPTER 11 GOSSIP

TAPESCRIPT

D. Choosing the Best Answer

1. Michael Jordan's teammates and friends were shocked to learn of his plans to retire from basketball less than a year after he had won the sport's top award and an Olympic gold medal. He had kept his decision secret until just before he made his announcement to the press.
2. When Clark Gable removed his shirt in a scene from a 1934 movie, audiences across the nation suddenly became alert and attentive. In fact, that scene attracted so much attention that sales of undershirts dropped sharply after the movie came out.
3. Most of his friends didn't like it much when Louis XIV of France visited them. He smelled terrible, as he never took a bath in his life.
4. Marilyn Monroe was killed because she associated with the wrong people. Her "friends" in the Mafia concluded that she knew too much and therefore was a threat to their organization.
5. Cuban dictator Fidel Castro worked as an actor during the early forties, performing in several hit movies, including *Holiday in Mexico*. Critics praised Castro's performance, saying that he displayed "exceptional talent."
6. The director of the space program in this country was terribly embarrassed when a reporter discovered that no astronauts had ever actually landed on the moon. The televised landings really took place in the Nevada desert.
7. A famous divorce lawyer in California once said that most marriage partners are only nice as long as things are going their way. If your marriage is failing, he can help you get a divorce *and* a lot of money. He set a United States record by winning a divorce settlement of $85 million for the ex-wife of a Saudi prince!
8. Although it was the French national anthem, no one challenged Napoleon when he banned the playing of "La Marseillaise" because of its revolutionary tone.
9. In 1992, the Prince and Princess of Wales, Charles and Diana, appeared in newspaper headlines everywhere by officially separating after many years of rumors that their marriage had failed.
10. Researchers at Harvard University have perfected a method of using mental telepathy to maintain contact with people who are miles away.
11. In 1978, twenty-three years after Albert Einstein's death, the American public was very surprised when it was revealed that the great scientist's brain lay forgotten in a container in the corner of a doctor's office in Kansas.
12. As King Henry VIII lay dying in his bed, he asked the attending physicians about his condition. Although it is certain the doctors knew he was dying, they reported that he was not seriously ill because it was considered high treason to predict a king's death.

ANSWER KEY

D. Choosing the Best Answer

1. b, T	5. b, F	9. c, T
2. a, T	6. c, F	10. c, F
3. c, T	7. b, T	11. a, T
4. c, F	8. a, T	12. a, T

E. Retelling the Story

These answers are provided as examples only; other answers are possible.

1. Dixie Ditz was happy that her listeners could drop in for a while.
2. "True or False?" is a show that claims to always have the last word.
3. Dixie just couldn't keep the rumors bottled up any longer.
4. Dixie was about to discuss a wide variety of topics and wanted her audience to get the picture.
5. Dixie predicted that Madonna's latest look would be out of this world.
6. She said there would be plenty of Madonna's male admirers who would come alive when they saw her.
7. Brian wanted to know if there were any fans of Elvis Presley who had stayed in touch with Elvis's spirit.
8. Dixie said that if the rumor were true, it would prove Elvis to be just a fairweather friend.

9. Another man asked if it was true that a large tobacco company was making waves by promoting the legalization of marijuana.
10. Dixie said she would be floored if that were true.
11. Dixie said that she must travel in the wrong circles, because she doesn't know any space aliens.
12. It is her opinion that those who tell stories about UFOs will have egg on their face when they find out the truth.

F. Putting the Idioms into Practice

These answers are provided as examples only; other answers are possible.

1. MAN DROPS IN AFTER EIGHT-YEAR DISAPPEARANCE
2. ACTIVIST ACCUSED OF BEING FAIRWEATHER FRIEND
3. GIRL KILLED BECAUSE OF TRAVELING IN THE WRONG CIRCLES
4. AUDIENCE COMES ALIVE AT SYMPHONY CONCERT
5. PROMINENT MEDICAL RESEARCHER HAS EGG ON HIS FACE
6. REINCARNATED HOUSEWIFE MAKES WAVES
7. REPUBLICAN CANDIDATE GETS THE LAST WORD
8. ENVIRONMENTALLY CONCERNED STUDENTS GET THE PICTURE
9. FAMOUS STAR KEEPS SECRET BOTTLED UP FOR OVER A YEAR
10. RECORD-BREAKING DIAMOND OUT OF THIS WORLD
11. COUPLE STAY IN TOUCH FOR MORE THAN FIFTY YEARS
12. LOCAL RESIDENT FLOORED BY BEAUTY QUEEN'S GRATITUDE

CHAPTER 12 ACHIEVING SUCCESS

TAPESCRIPT

D. Choosing the Best Answer

1. If you ever want to play a game of cricket, first you'll have to learn the ropes.
2. The party is less than a month away, and nobody has thought of a theme yet. We've got to get our gears turning.
3. I hope I don't get stuck in Ms. Telly's class. She always goes by the book.
4. You're going to have to prove that you can do this job. Here is a list of duties that I expect you to follow to the letter.
5. We can't get rolling on the rest of the house until the cement workers pour the concrete, and they are currently on strike.
6. This shampoo stacks up pretty well against the salon brand, and it's much cheaper.
7. Trevor's looking for a job again. He's apparently not worth his salt.
8. The Easton High School team has played middle-of-the-road football this year.
9. How can we lower our prices any more than we already have? We're about to go belly-up!

10. My mechanic can put any type of engine back together—no sweat!
11. I will never make it through the first semester in college. It's only the second week, and I'm snowed under!
12. I think you should talk to someone who won't give you the runaround. Here's my lawyer's number—why don't you give her a call?

ANSWER KEY

D. Choosing the Best Answer

1. b	5. b	9. a
2. b	6. a	10. b
3. a	7. b	11. b
4. a	8. b	12. a

E. Retelling the Story

These answers are provided as examples only; other answers are possible.

1. Before you start your own business, you should learn the ropes.
2. Next, you should get your gears turning to determine what you can do to compete with other businesses.
3. You don't always have to go by the book.
4. However, you should always follow government regulations to the letter.
5. Get rolling as soon as you can.
6. Be aware of how your product stacks up.
7. A successful businessperson is always worth his/her salt.
8. Never be content to be middle-of-the-road.
9. Your business will go belly-up if it is not competitive.
10. Tell your customers that you can do anything they want—no sweat.
11. You may be snowed under by all your work, but you should always treat your customers with absolute respect.
12. Your customers will not like it if you give them the runaround.

F. Putting the Idioms into Practice

1. learn the ropes
2. snowed under
3. get his gears turning
4. no sweat
5. middle-of-the-road
6. go by the book
7. get rolling
8. stacks up
9. has been getting the runaround
10. worth his salt
11. go belly-up
12. to the letter

CREDITS

The ads in this book are reprinted with the permission of the following companies or individuals:

Unit 1

pp. 1, 13 (top)	Isuzu Truck of America, Inc.
p. 12	Hunt-Wesson Inc. (Wesson is a registered trademark of Hunt-Wesson Inc.)
p. 13 (bot.)	American Gas Association
p. 14	U.S. Air Force
p. 15	AT&T

Unit 2

pp. 19, 28	Tiffany & Co.
pp. 29, 30	Toyota Motor Sales, U.S.A., Inc.
p. 31 (top)	Custom Concept
p. 31 (bot.)	Honeywell-Enviracaire
p. 32	The Church Ad Project

Unit 3

pp. 37, 48 (top)	Sea World, Inc.
p. 47	Avant
p. 48 (bot.)	Lego Systems, Inc.
p. 49	Nelson ad provided by Saturn Corporation is reproduced with permission of Saturn Corporation.
p. 50	Weider Food Companies

Unit 4

pp. 55, 68 (bot.)	Continental Airlines
p. 67	Colgate-Palmolive Company
p. 68 (top)	Thomas J. Lipton Co.
p. 69	Copyright (1993) Mazda Motor of America, Inc. Used by permission.
p. 70	ALLTEL Corporation
p. 71	Leonard Schwartz, M.D.

Unit 5

pp. 75, 86 (top)	® The Procter & Gamble Company. Used with Permission.
p. 85	Ministers Life Resources
p. 86 (bot.)	Colgate-Palmolive Company. Photo by James McLoughlin.
p. 87	Toyota Motor Sales, U.S.A., Inc.
p. 88	3 M Company
p. 89	American Gas Association

Unit 6

pp. 93, 104 (bot.)	Four Seasons Hotels, Ltd.
p. 103	Hewlett-Packard
p. 104 (top)	THK Photo Products, Inc. U.S. distributor of Tokina camera lenses.
p. 105	Principal Financial Group
p. 106	© Visa U.S.A. Inc.1992. All Rights Reserved. Reproduced with the permission of Visa U.S.A.
p. 107	The Army National Guard

Unit 7

pp. 111, 125	Helene Curtis Industries, Inc.
p. 122 (top)	Samsonite Corporation
p.122 (bot.)	Copyright 1985 Dow Jones & Company, Inc.
p. 123 (top)	De Beers
p.123 (bot.)	Longines-Wittnauer Watch Co.
p. 124	Continental Bank

Unit 8

pp. 129, 140	ClubHouse Inns
p. 141 (top)	State Farm Insurance Companies
p.141 (bot.)	ITT Sheraton Corporation
p. 142 (top)	Porsche Cars North America, Inc.
p.142 (bot.)	Brooks Sports Inc.
p. 143	McDonald's Corporation

Unit 9

pp. 147, 160 (top)	American Athletic Inc.
p. 158	The North Face, Inc.
p. 159	Illinois Bell
p. 159 (bot.)	California Egg Commission
p.160 (bot.)	Parker Brothers
p.161	The Church Ad Project

Unit 10

pp. 165, 179	Fieldcrest Cannon, Inc.
p. 176	Fisher-Price Toys, Inc.
p. 177 (top)	Toyota Motor Sales, U.S.A., Inc.
p. 177 (bot.)	Hershey Foods Corporation and Cadbury Limited
p. 178	Sheraton Grande Torrey Pines

Unit 11

p. 183, 196 (bot.)	Swiss Life
p. 195	Fantastic Foods, Inc.
p. 196 (top)	Michael Foods
p. 197	The Franklin Mint Corporation
p. 198	Stouffer Hotels and Resorts
p. 199	Palm Springs Convention and Visitors' Bureau

Unit 12

pp. 203, 213	Army materials provided courtesy of the U.S. Government, as represented by the Secretary of the Army.
p. 214	Chevron U.S.A. Products Company
p. 215	Toyota Motor Sales U.S.A., Inc.
p. 216	Mita Copystar America, Inc.
p. 217	Bank of America, © 1992 Bank America Corporation